MW00987813

CHANGE 101

ALSO BY BILL O'HANLON

Pathways to Spirituality

A Guide to Inclusive Therapy

A Brief Guide to Brief Therapy (with Brian Cade)

A Guide to Possibility Land (with Sandy Beadle)

An Uncommon Casebook (with Angela Hexum)

Even From a Broken Web (with Bob Bertolino)

In Search of Solutions (with Michele Weiner-Davis)

Stop Blaming, Start Loving (with Pat Hudson)

Rewriting Love Stories (with Pat Hudson)

Solution-Oriented Hypnosis (with Michael Martin)

Taproots

CHANGE 101

*A Practical Guide
to Creating Change
in Life or Therapy*

BILL O'HANLON

W. W. Norton & Company
New York • London

For information about permission to reproduce selections from
this book, write to Permissions, W. W. Norton & Company, Inc.,
500 Fifth Avenue, New York, NY 10110

Manufacturing by R.R. Donnelley-Harrisonburg
Book design by Charlotte Staub
Production Manager: Leeann Graham

Library of Congress Cataloging-in-Publication Data
O'Hanlon, William Hudson.
    Change 101 : a practical guide to creating change in life
or therapy / Bill O'Hanlon.
        p. cm.
    Includes bibliographical references and index.
    ISBN 978-0-393-70496-9
    1. Change (Psychology). I. Title: II. Title: Change one hundred
and one. III. Title: Change one hundred one. IV. Title: Practical
guide to creating change in life or therapy.

BF637.C4043 2006
158—dc22.   2006040128

ISBN 13: 978-0-393-70496-9
ISBN 10: 0-393-70496-3

W. W. Norton & Company, Inc.,
500 Fifth Avenue, New York, N.Y. 10110
www.wwnorton.com

W. W. Norton & Company Ltd.,
Castle House, 75/76 Wells St., London W1T 3QT

    2 3 4 5 6 7 8 9 0

To

Steffanie
my change agent and love of my life

AND

The Biscuit
opening my heart and changing me
in good ways on a regular basis

CONTENTS

ACKNOWLEDGMENTS

As usual, the crowd at Norton Professional Books: Deborah Malmud, Andrea Costella, Michael McGandy, Kevin Olsen, and all the other elves who work behind the scenes to make my leather into shoes. Thanks. I've listened and not listened, as in previous projects.

Milton Erickson, rider of the purple sage, for warping me early on to believe change was possible. And for confusing me so much that I was motivated to work out what you did for myself.

My clients, who, through the years, taught me much more than my professors and textbooks.

INTRODUCTION

INTRODUCTION

The greatest violence is when you attack
somebody with the notion that they're
hopeless; that they can't change.

—SEAN PENN

When I was a fledging therapist, in graduate school, I had a professor who made the pronouncement: The only person who really wants to change is a wet baby! I was dismayed and hoped that he was wrong in this view. I had, by that time, come across the work of a therapist who would turn out to be a big influence on my clinical work and life: the eccentric and creative psychiatrist Milton H. Erickson. Erickson had a different view of the process of change. In the introduction to the book *Change* (Watzlawick, Weakland, & Fisch, 1974), Erickson wrote about taking the seething forces of change inherent in individuals, couples, and families and channeling them in positive directions. Seething forces of change. That seemed more like it to me.

I had a personal stake in this clash of views. I had been miserable through much of my adolescence and early adult life and was desperately seeking methods of change that would help me be less unhappy. I had to believe change was possible. Being depressed, my life literally depended on finding such hope. Erickson provided such a hopeful, but also practical, framework. I swam toward the raft of Erickson's work like the drowning man I was. Indeed, many of the cases in this book are from Erickson's clinical work, since he knew more about how to help people change than anyone else I have ever met, and his cases are often dramatic illustrations of the principles of change in action.

I think people who seek therapy are like I was, hoping to find hope and some way out of the misery and suffering they are experiencing. Giving them the tacit message that change is not possible or might take many years of effort is to dash their hopes. At the same time, we have to provide effective means of realizing these hopes—they cannot be false hopes or ineffective methods.

This book, then, arises from these dual requirements—to find a hopeful view of the possibilities of change and to provide guidance in effective methods of creating change.

The first case I came across of Erickson's (O'Hanlon & Hexum, 1991) both baffled and excited me and clearly pointed to the possibility that people could change, even in desperate circumstances and even when they initially appeared uncooperative or difficult.

A woman entered therapy with Erickson and announced that she had definitive plans to kill herself in three months. She had thought about the matter a good deal and decided that her life was not worth living. Because she thought she should examine the issue as a rational matter before she made her final decision, she had decided to consult a psychiatrist to confirm her conclusion that nothing could be changed in her situation and that she had made the proper analysis. She was prepared to cooperate fully, but if Dr. Erickson should try to hospitalize her, she would merely pretend that she was sane and had given up her temporary notion of suicide and would then act on her plan without waiting.

Erickson agreed to see her, but with a condition of his own. She must agree to do everything he asked of her in therapy, unless, of course, it were unethical, illegal, or dangerous. She assured Erickson that she would accept his condition and that she was a person who could be counted on to keep her word.

Therapy began and Erickson discovered that the woman had been raised by parents who had clearly indicated to her that she was an accident and had gone on to provide only the bare minimum of care minus any warmth. They clothed and fed her, got her a basic education, and that was it. They never hugged her or expressed any affection to her. Her parents were entirely involved with each other and had no interest in her or anyone else. She had never known any of her relatives, since her parents had been distant from their families of origins. She had gone out on her own after high school and worked since then, seeing her parents occasionally, until, when she was in her mid-twenties, they had died in a car accident. Since then, she had drifted from one menial job to another, usually working as a secretary or receptionist, growing bored after a year or so and seeking out another similar job. She was in her late twenties when she entered therapy with Erickson. He found out she had $5,000 in savings (quite a bit in the early 1960s, when this therapy occurred) and that she had no one to leave her money to when she died. He suggested that she use some of her money to treat herself. He had noticed that she seemed to work hard to make herself unattractive—she wore unflattering clothes and no makeup. Erickson sent her out to get new clothes and makeup lessons. She did not see the point of it all, but Dr. Erickson reminded her of her agreement to do what he asked unless what he asked her to do was unethical, illegal, or dangerous. Soon she was looking better. He found out that she thought she was unattractive to the point of being repulsive and that she considered her most unattractive feature to be a small gap between her two front teeth. To Erickson, it seemed almost unnoticeable, but to her it seemed large and grossly visible to all who saw her smile. She tried hard not to smile or show her teeth. Erickson gave her the assignment of learning to squirt water through the gap in her teeth while she was taking a shower until she could squirt it with an accuracy of 8–10 feet.

Erickson found out two other things about her that he was soon to use in therapy. First, he learned that she had no happy memories in her life. He also discovered that, although she didn't recognize it, there seemed to be a young man at work who was interested in her. She told Erickson that whenever she went to the drinking fountain to get a drink of water, this young man would seem to magically appear and try to talk to her. She, of course, would quickly beat a retreat to her desk, fearing that the young man would see how ugly she was.

A month or so into the treatment, Erickson told the young woman he had come up with a plan to create one happy memory for her, since no one, in his opinion, should die without at least one happy memory. She considered this ridiculous and couldn't imagine, in her state, how she could ever have a happy experience.

Erickson outlined his plan to her as she grew more and more abashed. On the coming Monday, she was to get dressed up in her favorite new outfit, put on her makeup, and go to work. She was to go to the drinking fountain every hour. When the young man showed up, she was to get a mouthful of water, squirt the water at him, take one step toward him, and turn around and "run like hell." At first she balked at carrying out the task, but Dr. Erickson reminded her of her agreement to cooperate fully. This action, while difficult, was not unethical, illegal, or dangerous. Finally, she agreed to do it.

When the young man showed up at the drinking fountain, she did as instructed and ran away. The young man chased her, caught her, and playfully gave her a kiss. This began a whirlwind romance that led to her giving up all her notions of suicide.

When I read that case, I was both exhilarated and mystified. How did Erickson get his patient to do such an outlandish thing? How did he come up with the idea of using the gap in her teeth as part of the solution to her problem? How did he know it would work? The case clearly showed that people can change and they can change relatively quickly, but would I ever be able to do this kind of thing? The effect was electrifying and sent me on a quest that took many years, first to try to understand Erickson's insights into how people change and how to enlist them in the change process, and next to work out how I could apply these insights in my own practice and in my own life. The results of this personal and professional inquiry are contained in the pages of this book. I have included many personal anecdotes in the text. If you are a therapist, I hope you will enjoy this touch. If not a therapist, I hope you will at least tolerate it. Many of the lessons and methods I impart here have been tested in the proving ground of my own experience and I find it makes some of the examples more vivid. I have also included examples from Milton Erickson's work in the text. Since I learned so much from him about the process of change over the years, this also seems only fitting and I hope readers will appreciate these examples enough to investigate Erickson's work for themselves.

I have been a psychotherapist for over 30 years now and have studied most of the major approaches to therapeutic change, but more important, I have observed what has worked and not worked to produce change in therapy and in life over the 50 some years I have been alive.

I try to write my books in a way that is readable and simple, but hopefully not overly simplistic. Too many therapy books are filled with jargon and dense theories and often sit unread by the side of therapists' beds. I want mine to be read and used. I have heard from many therapists that their clients have read the books I have written for professional audiences and have gotten much out of them. I sincerely hope the material in this book is helpful for you and, if you are a therapist, helps those with whom you work.

CHANGE 101

CHAPTER ONE

Never Try to Teach a Pig to Sing:

Finding the Motivation and Energy to Change

If you want truly to understand something, try to change it. —KURT LEWIN

Therapeutic change does not happen in a vacuum. Someone must be motivated to seek therapy out and to make change. As we will discuss, this someone is not always the person who appears in the therapist's office, but nonetheless, *someone* must be willing to put forth some effort to seek out change and make it happen. In this chapter we will detail the most crucial prerequisite to change in therapy and life: energy and motivation.

THE ANATOMY OF MOTIVATION

Motivation is the starting place for change. Too often, people try to make change without motivation and this is reflected in the phrase in the chapter's title: Never try to teach a pig to sing, because it wastes your time and annoys the pig. People have to have energy to change, without energy the effort is a waste of time for all concerned.

If one considers human history, one can quickly discern that there are two main things that motivate human beings: things they want to avoid or get away from and things they desire or want to go toward. For convenience sake, let's call these two motivations *negative* (things people want to avoid or get away from or have less of in their lives) or *positive* (things people want more of or want and seek out or desire).

In this chapter, we will examine the variations on these two major themes. We will further divide these motivation types by time: past, present, and future. That leaves us with six variations on our two major motivational types:

Negative past motivation   Positive past motivation
Negative present motivation   Positive present motivation
Negative future motivation   Positive future motivation

Below are some signs and clues to look for to determine what point of view a client is operating from:

- If your client speaks mostly about the past (either what they disliked or what hurt them), they are likely motivated by *negative past motivation.*
- If your client speaks mostly about how good things used to be or returns time and again to the better past, they are most likely motivated by *positive past motivation.*

- If your client focuses on what he or she doesn't like in the present situation, they are likely motivated by *negative present motivation.*
- If your client speaks mostly about what is going well in the present, they are likely motivated by *positive present motivation.*
- If your client speaks in a fearful or worried way about bad things that might happen in the future or how their lives might decline, he or she is probably motivated by *negative future motivation.*
- If your client speaks in a hopeful way about how things might go or what they would like to have happen in their life, he or she is probably oriented to *positive future motivation.*

We will examine each of these in turn and give examples to illuminate them and then suggest how you might go about evoking or discovering which motivation will move your client.

NEGATIVE PAST MOTIVATION

I had a client who was told by his high school counselor not to bother applying to college because he wasn't really "college material." This pronouncement angered him. When he graduated from college, he dropped a note to that guidance counselor. And he sent another when he got his master's degree. And yet another when he finished his Ph.D. What do you think drove him through all the boring classes and tough reading and writing assignments in

the course of all that schooling? He was trying to prove
that counselor wrong about him and escape a curse from
his past.

This is a prime example of negative motivation arising
from the past. Typically, this variety of motivation comes
from something painful or unpleasant in our clients' pasts
that they are trying to avoid, correct, or get away from.

Sometimes people are motivated more by their
wounds than by their bliss.

Patsy Rodenberg coaches actors in finding and using
their voices. When interviewed, she was asked: Did you
ever have vocal problems growing up? She recounted
having a speech problem (she couldn't pronounce certain sounds) and being sent to an "elocution teacher"
who terrified the young Patsy. Patsy was never able to
achieve what the elocution teacher tried to get her to do.
She also had a stutter and was mocked by the other children. "Communication has always frightened me," she
said. "I don't think you could coach people with sympathy unless you had problems of your own."

This story illustrates another source of negative motivation from the past: being sensitized to one's own or
others' pain and turning that into energy to help others
or change the world in some way. I call this motivation
"follow your wound." What I mean by this is that if one
can use one's wounds as means to energize constructive
actions, even the negative can be a positive force.

Psychologist Sam Keen said it well: "We all leave childhood with wounds. In time we may transform our liabili-
ties into gifts. The faults that pockmark the psyche may

become the source of a man or a woman's beauty. The injuries we have suffered invite us to assume the most human of all vocations—to heal ourselves and others."

Steps to Access and Use Negative Past Motivation in the Change Process

1. Listen for the person's complaints, suffering, or wounds from the past. When one is mentioned, find out a bit more about the details and the emotion related to the incident or situation. Ask questions like: How does that incident or hurt motivate you in regard to the problem you brought in? What did you decide or learn from that previously hurtful situation that could help you through this difficult time?

2. Search for ways in which the person has made changes or stayed stuck related to the negative past events.

3. Link the proposed therapy activities—such as task assignments or discussions in the therapy room—and change to avoiding more of the kind of pain from the past that the person wants to get away from.

For example, a husband may be upset in couples therapy having to talk about the affair he had, as it is embarrassing for him. I might link this discussion to his motivation from a past hurt (his parents' divorce), and tell him that this discussion is important to help him and his wife avoid getting a divorce, which could cause pain for his children similar to the pain he suffered in his childhood.

Or I might link writing about a trauma each night for 15 minutes with the client's motivation to finally stop feeling pain from the trauma. I would tell the client that there is a fair amount of research showing that writing for as little as 15 or 20 minutes a day for as little as four days in a row can help diminish and resolve post-traumatic suffering.

POSITIVE PAST MOTIVATION

Sometimes people have motivation to reclaim or revisit something good from the past. There may have been a time when they had a sense of joy or peace or connection and they feel they have lost that in the present.

The solution-oriented approach to change is based in part on this motivation. In this approach, people are asked about what has worked in the past concerning present problems. Questions might be something like: Have you ever been depressed before and then somehow come out of it? If so, what did you do to come out of depression or how did you come out of it?

Steps to Access and Use Positive Past Motivation in the Change Process

1. Listen for the person's fond memories or best moments from the past. When one is mentioned, find out a bit more about the details and the emotion related to the incident or situation.

2. Search for ways in which the person has made changes based on what they remember or brought from the past positive situation or memory.

3. Link the proposed therapy activities—such as writing all he or she can remember about the positive past experience and what he or she learned from it or can use in the present difficult situation—and change to helping the person have more experiences like those of their past positive experiences.

For example, a client reported that her early childhood days, before she started school, were her happiest. She was asked to write about those days and what she remembered from them and then to extract from that writing some lessons or things she could use in her present difficulty (being overweight). The writing and thinking process that ensued led her to realize that she felt happy because she had no schedule in those years and could just follow her whims. She decided that she was overscheduled and overcommitted and this led to stress, which she coped with by overeating. She cut down on her commitments and was able to spend that free time doing more of what she pleased, which led to less "emotional" eating and more time to exercise.

NEGATIVE PRESENT MOTIVATION

Early in my therapy career, I had a job that was split between two different functions. In the afternoon I provided outpatient counseling. The other half of the time I answered the phones for the mental health center during evening hours in what usually turned out to be suicidal and other mental health crises. After some months on the job, I noticed something interesting—people on the phone in crisis changed much more quickly than people in outpatient counseling. The people on the phone were suffering right then and were searching for anything that would relieve that pain. They were more open to and motivated for change. By the time people arrived for appointments in outpatient counseling sessions, often their suffering was less acute and therefore they were less motivated to change. That is in part what attracted me to brief therapy—strike while the iron is hot and get people moving toward change as quickly as possible.

A few years later, I was hired to consult with an inpatient psychiatric hospital in my area. The hospital had hired a national consulting firm that informed the CEO at the end of the assessment that the trend was toward shorter stays in the hospital and that this hospital needed to reduce their average stay by 10 days to be in line with national averages. Since I was local and taught brief therapy, they asked me to do some follow-up consulting and training. I asked the staff and management to describe to me the typical course of treatment a new patient received. I was astonished to discover that most patients received no therapy during the first few days of their hospitalization. "Why not?" I inquired. "Oh, we give them some time to get used to being on the unit and we assess their current level of medication to find out whether or not it is appropriate during that first few days. Then we begin interventions."

I suggested an analogy. "If you arrived at a medical hospital with pain of an unknown origin and the staff just assigned you a bed and observed you and let you get comfortable in the hospital, how would you react?" They all agreed they would be upset and complaining. They would want relief and a diagnosis as soon as possible.

I told them they were dissipating most of the motivation that patients had when they arrived at the hospital. Patients are usually very upset when they arrive at a hospital and they are often motivated to change because they or others are suffering.

People are often motivated to change because they are uncomfortable or suffering in the present. Alcoholics' stories of hitting bottom are another example. Many say they hit the lowest point in their lives and then finally get enough motivation to go through the difficult process of stopping or reducing their alcohol overuse.

At one of my workshops, I was speaking about creating motivation for children by lovingly letting them experience the consequences of their actions. A man named Butch came up to me and told me his story. When he was about two years old, his father got a new job as a milkman. His father had received the shiny new milk truck on a Friday and had given Butch a ride on each of the weekend days. When Monday morning came around, Butch's father walked out the back door to get in his truck to begin his route. Butch wandered out behind him, unnoticed by his mother. When Butch saw his father about to start the truck to drive away, he said, "Go truck." His father said firmly, "No, Butch, go back in the house. You can't go with Daddy today. Daddy has to work." "Go truck," Butch said louder. Still his father urged him to go back inside and refused to let him in the truck. Butch began to throw a tantrum, stomping his feet and yelling, "GO TRUCK!" When Butch saw that his father was not relenting, he charged headlong into the stone wall next to the driveway. His skull split open and blood came gushing out. His father jumped out of the truck and called Butch's mother. They stanched the bleeding and Butch's mother took him to get stitches. Everything settled down for a few days. But around Friday of that week, when his parents had let down their guard, Butch tried the same stunt. He followed his father out into the driveway and began immediately to go into tantrum mode. "GO TRUCK!" he yelled. His father jumped up into the truck, looked Butch directly in the eye, and said, "It's your head," then drove away. As he looked back in the mirror, he saw Butch look at the receding truck, look at the wall, and seem to think for a moment, then walk back inside the house.

Milton Erickson used this negative present motivational method effectively in therapy many times. One of the most striking examples was the retired gentleman, Harlan, who sought Dr. Erickson's help for his severe insomnia. Erickson (O'Hanlon & Hexum, 1991) found out that Harlan tossed and turned all night every night, ever since his wife died, getting almost no sleep for weeks on end.

He would turn in early and look at the clock every fifteen minutes or so, trying his best to get to sleep. Erickson found out that Harlan lived in a large house with his son and that they both avoided the necessary task of hand-waxing the many wooden floors in their home. Erickson promised Harlan he could get him over his insomnia if Harlan would agree to cooperate with Erickson's plan. It would only cost Harlan eight hours of sleep. "Eight hours," Harlan replied. "I lose that much in one night."

Erickson's plan was simple. Harlan would go to bed at his usual bedtime (usually about 9 P.M.). If he could still see the clock in fifteen minutes, Harlan was to get up and wax the floors until his normal rising time (about 6 A.M.). The first night, as expected, Harlan spent the night waxing floors. The next night, although he was exhausted, he also waxed the floors all night. The third night, he began to wax the floors at 9:15 P.M., but soon grew so tired, he thought he would just rest for a little while before continuing. He quickly fell asleep and slept through the night. The next night, he also slept through the night, and every night thereafter until he saw Erickson for his next appointment. Harlan felt rather guilty about not completing the task on the third night, but Dr. Erickson told him that was fine. He also reminded Harlan that he still owed him two more nights of waxing if he were ever to experience insomnia again. But Harlan never did. Dr. Erickson joked: Harlan would do anything to avoid waxing the floors—even sleep all night!

My friend Margie used a similar method to motivate herself to lose weight. She really wanted to lose 15 pounds, but found herself continually losing a little weight and then putting it back on. After several years of this, she finally decided to get serious. She gave a check for her entire savings, $500, to a lawyer friend of hers. She was to appear at his office every Friday and weigh in. If she had not lost at least 1 pound that week, he was to mail the $500, along with a letter of praise for their work, to the KKK, an organization she despised. She lost the weight and kept it off. She wisely knew how to motivate herself by using negative present motivation.

Another case of Erickson's (O'Hanlon & Hexum, 1991) shows the importance of motivation in making change. A man sought Erickson's help to stop drinking alcohol to excess. In taking his history, Erickson asked the man whether he was married. The man answered, "Very married." He went on to explain that he and his wife were very close and spent several weeks each summer in their cabin in northern Arizona. They had only each other as company and, having stocked enough provisions, spent the two weeks totally nude, a freedom they both enjoyed. No one lived for miles around and they had total privacy. Upon hearing this, Dr. Erickson proposed a plan to help the man stop drinking. He and his wife should drive up to the cabin and clean out all the alcohol, giving it away or taking it back down to their home in Phoenix. Then they should have a friend of the man's wife drive them up to the cabin, drop them off, and take all their clothes, which the wife would bring out to the friend in the car. The friend was to return in two weeks with the car and the clothes. By then the man should have gone through detoxification and his craving for alcohol would be much diminished. Upon hearing the plan, however, the man decided he didn't really want to stop drinking after all. Erickson said ruefully when telling this story, "It would have worked. But your alcoholic has to be sincere."

Steps to Access and Use Negative Present Motivation in the Change Process

1. Ask the person what they don't like about their current situation and what they want to change.

2. Link any therapy tasks to changing that current situation about which they are unhappy.

POSITIVE PRESENT MOTIVATION

I was working with a couple and the husband expressed his reluctance to change. He said he thought he was incapable of changing; this was the way he was and that was that. I turned to him and asked a simple question: "Do you want to have more fun and nice times with your wife?"

"Of course," he answered.

"I will show you how to do that without changing who you are at core, but simply by doing a few things differently and speaking a bit differently to your wife."

"Okay," he answered simply, and that was the last I heard any objections from him during the therapy process. Once I'd tapped into his interests and reassured him that I was not going to make him over (defusing his negative future motivation), he was cooperative and motivated.

Again, Dr. Erickson (O'Hanlon & Hexum, 1991), always wise in the ways of motivation, provides a nice example of using this positive present motivation. One Saturday, his young son was complaining about having to do an unpleasant chore when he would have rather been playing. He had drawn the assignment of sweeping the basement floor. Dr. Erickson did not let him out of the task, but appeared at the top of the basement steps and watched his son listlessly sweeping the floor. It was obvious that his lackluster performance was extending the time it would take. Dr. Erickson spoke up and casually observed that the patterns that the push broom made in the dust reminded him of the advancing armies of the North and South during the American Civil War (which happened to be his son's passionate area of interest at the time). Then he walked away. When Dr. Erickson returned a few minutes later and glanced into the basement, he saw his son vigorously sweeping two lines of dust toward each other. The task was done in record time.

Steps to Access and Use Positive Present Motivation in the Change Process

1. Ask the person what is working or what they like about the current situation in the area they would

like to change. What I mean by this is that they are typically not unhappy about everything in their current life, just the problem parts. I often say something like, "We don't want to throw out the baby with the bathwater, so can you tell me about some parts of your life right now that *are* going well or that you like?"

2. Search for ways to expand the aspects of the situation that are working or that they like. For example, I might ask, "Can you find a way to have more of those parts of your life that are working now and less of the parts that aren't?" Or I might have them make a list of all the things they don't want to change in their current situation.

3. Mine the ways in which things are working for competencies or positive coping mechanisms to use in the change process.

NEGATIVE FUTURE MOTIVATION

The father of my colleague and first coauthor Jim Wilk practiced as a dentist in Chicago. After many years in the same location, he moved his office to another part of the city. Some years later, he was back in the neighborhood of his old practice and decided to visit the pharmacist who used to fill many of his patients' prescriptions. They had been professionally close but had lost touch after Dr. Wilk moved away.

When he stopped in at the pharmacy, however, there was a different pharmacist working at the counter. Dr. Wilk asked after his old colleague. The new pharmacist said that he was sorry to report that the man had died a year or so earlier.

"Gee, that's awful. He was my age. Do you know how he died?" asked Dr. Wilk.

"Yes, he had lung cancer. You know, he smoked for years," the pharmacist replied.

"Yes, I know he smoked. That smoking is a terrible thing," Dr. Wilk said, shaking his head.

"Yes it is," the pharmacist said. "Did you ever smoke?"

"I used to, but I quit," said Dr. Wilk.

"Oh, when did you quit?" the pharmacist asked.

"About five minutes ago," Dr. Wilk told the astonished pharmacist and walked out the door. He never smoked another cigarette.

He had glimpsed a negative future and became instantly motivated to change.

My client, Mary, couldn't decide whether to leave her marriage or not. She was miserable with her cold and rather verbally abusive spouse, but wasn't sure she wanted to leave. We had spent many months going back and forth. She was stuck. She couldn't leave and she couldn't stay. Finally, I proposed this scenario. "It's now five years from now and you have stayed in the marriage. How does that feel?"

She instantly said, "I'm getting out. The thought of five more years of this hell is not what I want."

"Okay," I said, "now imagine it is five years from now and you are out of the marriage. What's your sense of that?"

"Much better, even if I end up lonely," she replied.

I have done the same process, taking it out past five years to much farther in the future ("Okay, you're 90 years old and . . .") when the shorter time frame didn't provide clarity or motivation to change.

A young man who was using barbiturates was living with his friend, another barbiturate user and a dealer. Over the months living with this dealer, the young man observed that the dealer often neglected to feed his young child and his pets. The young man cared deeply about children and pets and this began to bother him. One day, it struck him that if he continued his drug use, he might turn out to be the kind of person who cared more for the drugs than for children and pets. This became the impetus for him to stop using barbiturates.

Similarly, a methamphetamine user saw the father of her child die of an overdose and this became her impetus to enter a drug rehabilitation program.

A woman once appeared in my therapy office for an evening appointment wearing sunglasses. She told me that she would not remove her sunglasses because her face was bruised underneath them. She had been beaten by her boyfriend. All of her friends, her parents, his parents, and even her minister (she belonged to a church that frowned on divorce) had urged her to leave this violent relationship because they feared for her life. Her boyfriend had broken several of her ribs and her nose in previous battering incidents. What all these people did not really understand, she explained to me, was that he was a good man and they were deeply in love. She *couldn't* leave him. She supposed I would tell her she had to leave. I replied that she already knew that was the sensible move and had heard that advice, so I wouldn't bother to repeat it.

Why had she come to see me? I asked. The recent incident had frightened her more than the others because it had occurred around her daughter and her daughter had almost been injured when her mother fell onto a table near the daughter. She had decided to get some counseling. We talked about how much she loved both her daughter and her boyfriend. We talked about the likely future for both her daughter and her boyfriend. We agreed that her boyfriend, if he continued to be violent with her, would most likely end up killing her and going to prison. Her daughter, we decided, would grow up without a mother perhaps, or perhaps she would be injured in one of the violent episodes, or she might well grow up to be in a relationship with a person who was physically violent.

After this conversation, I told her that I believed she loved her boyfriend and her daughter, but I wasn't sure she loved them enough. She protested that she did. I told her that I believed her boyfriend could stop his violence but that he would be unlikely to do so without sufficient motivation. She knew that the main thing that would motivate him to change was the possibility of her leaving him (she had left him once before and he had stopped his violence for quite a while, but then she had stayed with him after another violent incident). She agreed to go back home and tell her boyfriend that she loved him and believed in him so much that she was willing to leave him to help him get his act together. If he ever got violent again or even threatened it, she would leave him and never return. He agreed and was nonviolent for about 6 months. Then he was violent again and she left him. When her resolve would waver, she would remind herself of the negative futures both her daughter and boyfriend would likely face if she relented.

Steps to Access and Use Negative Future Motivation in the Change Process

1. Discover what "futures" the person does not want to have happen or wants to avoid.

2. Link any therapy homework assignments to avoiding those unwanted or feared futures.

For example, a client who wanted to get his wife to consider reconciling because she was considering divorce was asked to balance his checkbook—a task he hated—and complete his late tax return before his wife was scheduled to file for divorce (a week from the time the assignment was given). He agreed because his opposition to divorce was greater than his opposition to these unpleasant tasks. His wife was upset with

him in part due to his financial irresponsibility, so
these actions were likely to motivate her to reconsider
divorce.

3. Ask the person what actions he or she would have to
   take in the near future to ensure that such a feared
   or unwanted future would not happen.

POSITIVE FUTURE MOTIVATION

James Stockdale, senior officer in the North Vietnamese
prisoner of war camps during the Vietnam War, tells of
the prisoners who lost hope and gave up during their
imprisonment. "The optimists didn't make it," he said.
They were the ones who believed that the prisoners
would be liberated by Thanksgiving. Then Thanksgiving would come and go. Then they would decide Christmas was the date and then Christmas would come and
go and they would set their sights on Easter. By the next
Thanksgiving, they would give up and often die. Stockdale said the way to keep going was to never give up
faith that they would eventually be liberated but not get
too attached to a particular date. He was speaking
about using the positive future to remain motivated in
the present.

Steps to Access and Use Positive Future Motivation
in the Change Process

1. Find out what "futures" the person would really like
   to have happen.

2. Work backwards from such desired futures to the present. Ask the person what he or she would have to do in the near future to lead toward one of those desired futures. Have the person list those things that would be happening in such a future and then create a step-by-step list that might lead to the desired future.

For example, a client who was shy very much wanted to have more friends. When I asked her what a future with friends looked like, she said that she would be going out to movies once a week with a friend or friends, she would be having meals with friends several times a week, and she would go to a party at least once a month and talk to someone new.

I asked her if she had any friends now who would be likely to go to a movie or out to a meal with her. She had one friend who liked movies, but preferred the early, discounted movie, which was difficult for my client to attend because the movie usually started soon after she got out of work. Through the course of our discussion, she decided that she could ask a coworker to cover for her last half-hour by agreeing to come in early and cover the first half-hour of the coworker's time.

We followed a similar tack for each of the other elements of her desired future, and soon she was having several meals with friends every week and going to the movies with a friend once a week.

3. Link the proposed therapy activities and change to getting the person to have more experiences like those of the past positive experiences. Get him or her to try some experiments and brainstorm how to overcome barriers or problems in implementation.

WHO IS MOTIVATED?

A man of about 67 years of age appeared in my office for his first appointment. "What brings you here?" I asked.

"My insurance man told me you could make me stop smoking."

"He was wrong," I replied. "I've never made anyone stop smoking."

"He said you could use hypnosis and make me stop."

"Hypnosis doesn't really make people stop smoking, but it might help them stop. Let me ask you this question, though. Do you want to stop smoking?"

"Not really," he replied.

"Well, then, we may be able to make this short. Why did you come in today?"

"Because my insurance man thought I should quit smoking."

He went on to tell me a story. When he discharged from the U.S. Navy in 1946, they had told him that he drank and smoked so much, they predicted he would be dead within ten years. Yet he had continued to drink until his doctor told him in 1980 that he would have to quit. He promptly quit drinking. Then a few years later, his doctor had told him that he must cut out fatty foods. He had also complied with this directive. He told me he used to enjoy a steak and glass of scotch each night, followed by cigarettes. Now the cigarettes were his only pleasure.

"Has your doctor told you to quit?"

"No," he said, "he told me it would be better if I quit, but he didn't say I had to quit."

"Well, if he did, would you stop?"

"Yep."

"Well, then I don't think you need hypnosis. If your doctor says it's time to stop, you'll most probably stop. If you have a tough time doing that, I would be happy to see you then. But for now, I think I'll just wish you a good day and tell you it was nice to meet you and no charge for this short meeting. You might consider telling your insurance man to mind his own business."

He stood up, shook my hand, and said, "You're a wise young man. Thank you." And off he went.

To begin therapy, it is important to identify and have access to the motivated person, that is, the person who is pushing for or desires change. Sometimes that person is not the person who shows up in your office or treatment setting. This doesn't necessarily mean that you cannot do therapy if the person who shows up is not motivated initially.

When I worked at community mental health centers, I used to have court-ordered clients who would arrive at my office angry at being sent to therapy and claiming not to have a problem. I learned after a few disastrous cases to respond quickly. "Fine," I would say as I stood up. "I will write a letter to the court (or your probation officer) and tell them you said you didn't have a problem and would rather go to jail than to have therapy. Good-bye." As I was walking toward the door, most would say, "Wait. I do have a problem." As I turned to face them, I would say, "Now I'm not sure if you are just saying that to stay out of jail or whether you really have a therapy-type problem." They would spend the next few minutes detailing the nature of their problem. My wife, formerly a therapist, said it succinctly: If you're the therapist, never be the most motivated person in the therapy room.

A case of mine illustrates this well. I saw a 12-year-old boy with his family because he had stopped going to school. He would be dropped off at school by his mother each morning but then would sneak away and spend the day just sitting bored on the roof of his family's apartment building. He did not really have an explanation for this, but just felt he could not go to school. He was not being bullied, he was a pretty good student, he wasn't generally rebellious. He had some friends at school. He was a likeable kid and the school had given him many "second chances." They finally referred him for therapy. For the next month or so, I tried everything I knew to both get to the bottom of the situation and work out why he was avoiding school and get him going again, to no avail. I spent hours consulting colleagues and reading books in search of something that might help me with this child. Finally, I received a call from the school informing me that the boy would have to be held back to repeat the school year if he didn't come to school and not miss a day beginning Tuesday. I met with the family on Monday evening and confessed my mystification and disappointment at not having helped them. I told them what the school had told me and apologized for not being more effective.

The boy went to school the next day. When I spoke to him later in the week, he explained that he kept expecting me to figure out why he wasn't going to school. When he finally realized he would have to repeat the grade and that I wasn't going to figure it out, he decided he would just make himself go to school. I just about fell off my chair and wished I had "given up" much sooner.

CREATING MOTIVATION

Of course, even if the person who shows up for therapy isn't initially motivated, therapists (or parents or workplaces or schools or governments) can create the context for motivation. Butch's father in the story above created a context for Butch to be motivated to stop throwing tantrums. Al-Anon provides coaching for spouses, family members, and friends of people who drink or use drugs excessively. They are coached to stop standing in front of the wall for the substance-abusing person and let them take the consequences of their destructive behavior. They are also coached to stop making excuses for the person (like calling in sick for the person when he or she is really drunk or hungover).

In order to create motivation, the therapist must have access to the client's friends and family and be aware of their "environment"—school, workplace, or other contexts that can provide positive or negative consequences for the client. Arrange with the people around the client to offer the client consequences (both positive and negative) that support their desired and undesired behaviors.

This technique has been used with drug and alcohol abusers for many years. Setting limits and providing consequences for drug or alcohol abuse and related behaviors can help increase the negative motivations in the present. If the partner of an abuser says they will move out of the house or the relationship if the person drives under the influence one more time can provide the needed push for the person to either get help or make a change.

Below is a summary of the steps involved in creating motivation:

1. Identify the situation or behavior that the client would like to change.

2. Find something about that situation or behavior that the client would consider either enjoyable and desirable, or abhorrent and undesirable.

3. Have the client's family and friends (those who have the power to create and deliver consequences) provide the desirable or undesirable consequences,

depending on how the client would like to approach the change.

For example, a client was drinking to excess quite often and his friends, coworkers, and family became concerned. His wife spoke to him but he denied that there was a problem. His wife then spoke to his coworkers and they agreed that they saw signs of problematic drinking. So, together, they came up with a plan. The coworkers, with whom the client occasionally traveled or went out for drinks after work, each approached him privately at one time or another and expressed their concern with his frequent drinking. After a few weeks of this, he approached his wife and said that he did indeed think he had a problem with alcohol and asked her help to find treatment.

LINK THE MOTIVATION TO THE DESIRED CHANGE

Once you find motivation, you need to link the motivation with the desired change.

Joan, who had lost her children when they were removed from her home, was angry at Child Protective Services (CPS) and refused to cooperate with their treatment plans. CPS had decided she was unmotivated and in denial. When I consulted on the case, Joan and the CPS worker assigned to her case were at odds. CPS thought Joan was codependent. Joan disagreed. They had been arguing about the nature of the problem while

the children languished in foster care, complaining that
they wanted to live back home with their mother.

I asked the CPS worker what had led to the children
being taken away. She said that Joan had been leaving
her young children at home alone and going to bars with
men friends. Neighbors would call the police and the
police would take the children into custody. This had
happened several times for brief periods until the last
incident, when CPS made an effort to permanently
remove the children from Joan's custody. Then Joan had
requested that CPS give her a chance to change. I told
the CPS worker that I assumed that the ultimate goal in
the situation was to ensure that the children were safe
and cared for. She agreed. I asked Joan whether she
agreed that it was important for the children to be safe
and cared for. She agreed. I asked the CPS worker what
would reassure her that Joan was either taking care of
the children or making certain they were cared for if she
wasn't directly caring for them. She said that it would
entail either Joan being home with them or having a
responsible adult care for them. I asked Joan whether or
not she was really motivated to get her kids back. She
said she was. I told her that the way she could show her
sincerity was to stop going to bars and leaving her children alone or to arrange for a responsible friend or family member to be with the children if she were not there.
She would also have to agree that the CPS worker could
stop by randomly to ensure that Joan was following
through. She said to me, "I could get my kids back if I

did this?" After conferring with the CPS worker, she agreed that Joan could have her children back if things went according to plan for a two-month trial period. Joan quickly agreed.

Joan was motivated to get her kids back. Once she understood what was required of her, she agreed to cooperate. She wasn't really interested in participating with codependency treatment, but she was interested in doing what it would take to get her children back.

WHAT TO CHANGE AND HOW TO IDENTIFY THE FOCUS OF CHANGE

Often beginning therapists will ask how they will know what to focus the change process on. The simple answer is: Focus on what is bothering the client or whoever referred the client. I joke that we therapist give our clients problems. Clients arrive only with concerns and complaints or carrying someone else's concerns and complaints. We help shape those concerns, complaints, and suffering into problems. That shaping process is influenced by our theories, methods of information gathering and assessment, and our own personal sensibilities. I, of course, suggest that therapists do their utmost to shape the raw dough of the complaints into solvable problems, but again there is a simple way of assessing whether you have hit on the correct beginning concern. Ask those who are motivated (clients or referrers) how they will know when the therapeutic change has occurred. What will satisfy them that they have arrived at the place in which the desired outcome or change has been reached?

In fact, I usually start therapy with a question about that final goal: "How will you know when you have gotten what you came for?" Or, if they have been sent by some-one else (the courts, their probation officer, their parents, their employer): "How will they know that you have made the changes they want you to make here?" I might follow this up with some specifics like: "What will you be doing differently after the change has been made?" "What will others notice that would show them this change without you even mentioning it to them?"

If clients bring multiple issues or concerns, I either ask them which is most pressing or try to find some theme that connects the disparate issues. For example, a client told me he drank to excess too often and also got into fights regularly. We agreed that what tied the two prob-lems together was that he was drinking when he got into fights and that he would act on impulse in both drinking too much and getting into fights. We agreed that drink-ing was the main issue upon which we would focus. This would help him not only stop fighting but, in several other areas as well, not to act on unhealthy impulses.

How would this go in a typical therapy session? Con-sider this sample dialogue from a first session:

Therapist: What brings you here?
Client: I can't sleep. I toss and turn all night.

Th: I assume you have pursued medical help and other solutions. What happened with those and what do you hope you can get out of therapy that will help you sleep?

Cl: Oh, yeah, I've been the medical route. I have taken prescriptions but they don't really work. I went to a sleep clinic last month and stayed overnight. Nothing came of that either. I thought maybe you could hypnotize me and make me sleep.

Th: Well, we'll see. I need to know a bit more first. When we are successful, though, how much will you be sleeping? That is, what are you going for as a result here? What would satisfy you in terms of what we accomplish together?

Cl: If I could get even six hours of sleep a night, that would be okay with me. I haven't slept more than one or two in the last two years. Seven or eight hours would be great.

In terms of our classification scheme in this chapter, this client has a negative present motivation. He wants to get away from the current problem of insomnia. One could also say he has a positive future motivation—getting at least six hours of sleep each night.

In some models of therapy and change, this presenting complaint would not set the problem definition. Those practitioners would search for another, underlying problem of which the insomnia may be a mere symptom or surface manifestation. But in the end, the client probably won't be satisfied that relevant change has occurred unless he is getting six hours of sleep a night, regardless of the therapist's conceptions. Ignore this motivation or insert another agenda at the peril of client satisfaction.

Here's another scenario that illuminates motivation.

Therapist: Your company referred you to me through your employee assistance program and all I heard is that you are having trouble with your supervisor.

Client: Yes, I'm not really sure if I am the one who should be here, though. My boss is a control freak. She second-guesses everything I do. She's always checking up on me, hovering over my shoulder, glancing at the computer screen, going through my phone messages when I am out to lunch. I grew up with a controlling, paranoid father and she's just like him. When I complained to my coworkers, one of them told her about what I said and boom, I end up seeing the EAP [Employee Assistance Program] counselor. Why didn't she send my boss to you for help. She's the one with the problem.

Th: Okay, so whether you're the right person to be here or not, you have a sense that if you didn't come to see me, your job might be in jeopardy, I assume.

Cl: Damn straight. I think my boss would fire my ass if she could without getting sued.

Th: So, if we decide to work together, you want to get your boss to be less controlling and you want to keep your job secure. If I can help you with either

or both of those things, you might think it is worth
seeing me, even if the problem is primarily your
boss's?

Cl: Yeah, I guess so. You think you could change my
boss without her coming in here?

Th: Maybe.

Cl: Well, sign me up then. I'm skeptical but that would
be great. I actually like the job and some of my
coworkers a lot and if it weren't for her controlling,
I would be happy there.

In this case, the client was referred by someone else
and has a past negative motivation, avoiding being controlled like he was in childhood. He also has, as most
clients have, a negative present and future motivation—
having his boss be less controlling and not losing his job.

FINDING A FOCUS IN THERAPY

I basically consider three major elements when I am trying to find the focus for change in therapy: the complaint, the customer or complainant, and the goal for
treament. Here are some questions to ask yourself to
clarify these three areas.

The Complaint(s)—What is bothering clients enough to
get them to seek therapy or get sent to treatment?

- Who is complaining?
- Who is alarmed about something?
- What are they complaining or alarmed about?

- How can you translate vague and blaming words into concrete action descriptions (videotalk)?
- When has the complaint typically occurred?
- Where has the complaint typically occurred?
- What are the patterns surrounding or involved in the complaint?
- How does the person, the customer, or others involved in the situation explain the complaint?

The Customer(s)/Complainant—Who is willing to pay for therapy and/or do something to effect change? Whose concerns will constrain or affect therapy? Who is pushing for change?

- Who is paying you?
- Who is complaining the most?
- Who will be able to terminate therapy?

The Goal(s)—How will the client(s) or customer(s) know when therapy has been helpful enough to terminate or when the agreed-upon results have been achieved?

- What are the first signs that will indicate (or already have indicated) progress toward the goal(s)?
- What are the final actions or results (again in videotalk—seeable, hearable, checkable, if possible) that will indicate that this is no longer a problem?
- How will we know when therapy is done, when it has been successful?

- In videotalk, explain what the goal is. Translate labels or theoretical concepts into action descriptions if possible. If not, get the client to rate the subjective experience of the problem on a scale and select a target number for success on that scale.

I also use some basic orienting questions when I begin therapy. You can ask clients these questions to orient yourself in the beginning of the change process.

1. What brings you here or concerns you (or whoever suggested you come see me)?

   This is sometimes called "determining the customer." It also clarifies the complaint that drove someone to seek or recommend therapy. If the therapist does not find this out and keep it in mind during the treatment, it usually indicates that the therapist believes that his or her theories about the person's or family's issues is more important than the clients'.

2. What do you (or they) want as a result? What will show you and others that that result has been achieved?

   This helps define a stopping point for successful therapy according to clients' definitions, rather than therapists' values and agendas. The question about showing self and others is important because it is hard to know when it is time to stop if it isn't defined in a clearly observable way.

3. What has worked in regard to your concern and
   what hasn't? This could include past help you have
   received or past attempts by you or others to resolve
   your concerns.

   This information helps avoid mistakes from the past
   and helps to focus on what things have helped and
   what is important to change.

What I have written in this chapter points to the idea that
unless you have motivation—juice—in therapy or in life,
you are not going to create change because there is no
fuel, drive, or pull to make change. And trying to make
change happen without motivation is like trying to teach
a pig to sing. It won't work, it wastes your time, and it
annoys the pig.

SOME QUESTIONS TO ASK CLIENTS TO IDENTIFY AND ELICIT MOTIVATION

What would you like to change or have be different
in your life?

What is the most pressing issue for you or your family
right now?

What could we change that would make the most
difference?

What has caused you pain or frustration in the past
that you want to make sure does not happen again?

What happened to you that you are adamant should
never happen to others?

What injustice or indignity did you suffer that sensi-
tizes you to others' similar pain or suffering? What
might that sensitivity lead you to do to use it in a
productive way?

What aspect of your life in the past are you longing
to re-create or stay connected to?

About what are you so uncomfortable at the moment
that you are motivated to change it?

What would you most like to change in your life or
situation right now?

If what's bothering you right now were resolved,
how would your life change?

If your fondest dreams came true, where would you be
and what would you be doing in a year? Five years?
Ten years? [Or choose an appropriate time frame.]

If things continue as they are going, what would be
happening in a year and how would that be for
you? Five years? Ten years? [Or choose an appropriate time frame.]

MOTIVATION 101: A SUMMARY

• You need to have energy and motivation to change.

• There are two types of motivation: things you want
to get away from and things you want to go toward.

• Identify which of these motivations is relevant for
your clients.

• If clients you are seeing are not motivated (a rarity—
they are often at least motivated to stop seeing

you or avoid legal consequences), find out who are motivated in the situation and tap into them for change.

• Link the identified motivation to the desired change. [Note: This almost always involves finding a future positive or negative motivation.]

CHAPTER TWO

The Journey of 1,000 Miles:

The Small-Steps Method of Change

True life is lived when tiny changes occur.
—LEO TOLSTOY

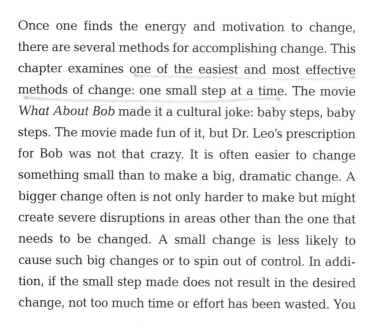

Once one finds the energy and motivation to change, there are several methods for accomplishing change. This chapter examines one of the easiest and most effective methods of change: one small step at a time. The movie *What About Bob* made it a cultural joke: baby steps, baby steps. The movie made fun of it, but Dr. Leo's prescription for Bob was not that crazy. It is often easier to change something small than to make a big, dramatic change. A bigger change often is not only harder to make but might create severe disruptions in areas other than the one that needs to be changed. A small change is less likely to cause such big changes or to spin out of control. In addition, if the small step made does not result in the desired change, not too much time or effort has been wasted. You can always try another method of change or another small step can be made. If the change is in the right direction, one can easily add to or expand on it.

The same applies to changing established habits. Sometimes one can stop a habit all at once, but as Mark Twain said, more often it is a matter of making small changes: "Habit is habit and not to be flung out of the window by any man, but coaxed downstairs a step at a time."

Writing a book can be a challenging and long process and sometimes we authors wonder if it is worth it all. But every once in a while, we have an experience that convinces us it is indeed worth it.

After a previous book of mine was released, it was featured on *Oprah*. After that show aired, I received an e-mail from a woman who had viewed the program and bought the book as a result. She told me that she had a drug problem and wondered if I could steer her to someone in her area who worked in the way the book described (solution-oriented therapy). I happened to know three different therapists who worked in that way in her area and I gave her their names.

After a year of not hearing from her, I got an e-mail that told me her story. Years before, she had been a heroin addict, living on the streets. She had stopped using drugs when she became a born-again Christian. She had gotten a job as a secretary in the church at which she had converted and for some years had a comfortable life. She would testify to the power of Jesus by telling her story frequently in her church, so everyone knew she had been a drug addict.

Several years prior to her contacting me, she began to have severe and persistent back pain, for which she finally had surgery. She had become addicted to the painkillers she was prescribed postsurgery and had begun buying illegal pain pills on the street. When she had seen me on television, she was using up to 27 pills per day. She felt as if she couldn't tell anyone at her church, since she might lose her job and since they might be disappointed that her Christianity no longer kept her immune from drug problems.

After calling the therapists whose names I had given her, she decided that, with the financial problems she had due to the expense of purchasing the illegal drugs, she couldn't really afford therapy. So she decided to reread my book and use the principles to see if she could solve the problem herself. The book, *Do One Thing Different*, had a simple premise—change one small thing in order to make a big change in your life.

She began to shave a little off of her 27th pill each day, figuring that she wouldn't notice such a small change. It worked. Each day, she shaved a little more off the pill until she was taking 26. She repeated the process for 8 months until she was able to stop taking the pills all together. She wrote me to tell me of her success and to thank me. Aside from how moved I was, I thought it was a good example of the take-small-steps approach to change.

SMALL ACTIONS

Colleen, a client of mine, was in the midst of a nasty divorce. Her soon-to-be ex-husband had convinced the children at the last minute to cancel their plans to spend Thanksgiving with her and to attend Thanksgiving with him at his parents' house. Colleen was stuck with a large turkey and the depressing prospect of facing a miserable Thanksgiving alone. We had previously discussed her attending a support group. She had attended one session and decided the group was not for her since she couldn't relate to anyone else. I had told her at the time that there was an informal policy in AA that you should attend at least three times before you decide it is not for you and had encouraged her to try the same policy with the support group. That Thanksgiving morning Colleen decided to see if any of the neighbors in her apartment building might want to join her for dinner. There was no answer at the first door when she knocked and she almost ran back to her apartment, but then she remembered our discussion about trying three times before giving up. To Colleen's surprise, the next door she knocked on was answered and led to a couple agreeing to come to dinner with her. She then knocked on more doors and ended up having seven people over for a nice meal. New to the apartment building, she made friends with some of them that day, and these relationships became a source of support in the difficult months that lay ahead.

When I coach to people to write books, I suggest they start with small writing sessions, as little as five minutes. Almost no one can credibly claim they don't have such a short period in their busy lives to write, so most follow through on this small commitment. Of course, once they begin writing, they almost always write for more than five minutes, but even if they didn't, writing five minutes per day will eventually get the book written.

I used to procrastinate doing difficult tasks, like preparing my records to do my annual income tax. After several years of this, I finally came up with a method that worked for me. Previously, I would have an unorganized mess of papers, some of which were related to my tax filings and some of which weren't. I decided I would spend five minutes (seems to be a magic number, doesn't it?) once a week merely sorting papers. I created one stack of tax-related papers and one stack on non-tax-related papers. Once the tax stack was completed, usually after several weeks, I began another sorting process five minutes per week, creating small piles with each broad tax category, such as income for one and expenses for another. From there, I would create file folders with different categories of expenses and income during my 5-minute sorting sessions. For the first time in the year I implemented this system, I got my taxes completed on time. In subsequent years, I created my filing system at the first of the year and the records became more organized from the start. There were still those stacks of unorganized papers but I had my method, and they took only a few weeks to sort through.

Below is a list of strategies therapists can use to lead their clients to small-action steps:

1. Identify the situation or problem the client wants to change.

2. Get the client to commit to a series of experiments, trying first one small change, then another, until one makes a positive difference.

3. If the person is highly motivated, suggest changes in actions first. If they are not so motivated, first suggest changes in point of view or focus of attention, or enlist someone else in the person's life to make small changes.

For example, a client of mine developed a habit of picking at small flaws on her face (or other parts of her skin). She found this irresistible and although she wanted to stop, she couldn't. Her boyfriend was then enlisted to help. She asked him to hide the small magnifying mirror she used in this activity, so she would have to approach him to get it when she felt compelled to pick her skin. She was reluctant to do this, even though the boyfriend had never berated her or tried to stop her from doing this. In the end, enlisting her boyfriend's help in this small way dramatically reduced her obsessive behavior.

To implement this small-action-steps method, ascertain from your client the smallest action they could and—this is important—*would* agree to take in the problem area.

Here's an example from a therapy session:

Client: Whenever I talk to my parents, I get really upset.

Therapist: What's the smallest change you think you could do that might change the situation?

Cl: I don't know. I don't think I can do anything. They're just the way they are. They'll never change. They have never approved of what I do. Every time I try to tell them something positive that happened, they either tell me why it's not that great or what could go wrong in the future.

Th: Well, then maybe you could turn the tables. Take the initiative by telling them something good and then immediately tell them what might go wrong with it in the future and why it's not that big a deal. Beat them to the punch and it might shift the conversation.

Cl: I never thought of that. I would have to think about it ahead of time. They are so good at it and I am almost always surprised with what they come up with. Like with some things, I start the conversation, sure that this time they will be really happy for me and there is nothing they could come up with that would undermine that. But they always do.

Th: Maybe you could practice with a friend. Role-play. You do your part and have your friend do your parents'.

Cl: That might work. If I could beat them to the punch, I would feel as if I were in control. It could even be fun trying to come up with their part and then leaving them with nothing to do but agree with me.

SMALL SHIFTS IN VIEWPOINT OR FOCUS

Roger Bannister ran the first sub-4-minute mile. Bannister and several other runners around the world were getting close to breaking the 4-minute-mile barrier, but none of them, despite repeated efforts, could seem to accomplish the goal. Many came to believe that since the best runners could not accomplish it, it was beyond the capacity of the human body. Bannister was worried about this possibility, but he found a way to "trick" himself out of it. He decided not to focus on running a sub-4-minute mile, but only to attempt to run a sixteenth of a second faster each time he competed. He knew that this was possible. After several competitions with this new focus, he finally broke the 4-minute barrier. Incidentally, after he broke the barrier, several of his competitors also did within the next year.

A woman had been struggling with compulsive eating most of her life. She had the typical all-or-nothing mentality that often accompanies eating problems. She came across the idea of small shifts in perception and decided it would be helpful for her. She began to shift her attention in a small but significant way. Each time she criticized herself internally for overeating, she would recall the entire week, rather than her last eating incident. With this broader perspective, she would relax and realize that since her eating had been relatively good all week, she didn't need to panic about gaining weight. This realization helped prevent future episodes of overeating, since she was not so upset or panicked.

A client of mine who was prone to depressive episodes used a similar strategy. I asked her to describe her thinking and focus of attention both during depressive episodes and when she was emerging from them and starting to feel better. She discovered that there was a crucial difference. When she was feeling very depressed, she would think negative and fearful thoughts about the future ("I'll be like this forever. I will probably have to be hospitalized or move back in with my parents because I won't be able to function on my own or earn a living."). In contrast, when she was feeling better or coming out of the deepest part of the depression, she would begin to think about some small (or not so small) thing she had accomplished in the recent past. Even if it was something like, "Well, I got up out of bed and brushed my teeth today," that seemed to be enough to help her feel better about her life and herself. We made a plan that for the next week, since she was currently feeling very depressed, she would find one thing each day that she could give herself credit for. She tried it and found that it set off a cascading series of positive developments for her. When she found the thing she could give herself credit or praise for, she had a little burst of energy. With this burst of energy, she was often able to do something else that helped her challenge her depressed feelings, hopelessness, or isolation, like calling a friend or doing some artwork.

Here's a sample from a therapy session that shows this aspect of the small-change method:

Client: I think I'm really selfish.

Therapist: Well, there's selfish and then there's selfish.

Cl: What do you mean?

Th: Well, one kind of selfish is when a person takes advantage of others and thinks only of oneself. Another kind of selfish is when a person cares for oneself or takes care of oneself, but doesn't necessarily take advantage of others or refuse to help others.

Cl: Well, I guess I'm the second kind. I don't take advantage of other people or treat them badly. I guess I feel a little guilty when I do things for myself.

Th: Okay, so I wouldn't call that selfish. I'd call that guilty. Has there been a time when you did take care of yourself and felt okay about it?

Cl: I guess a couple of times.

SMALL COMMITMENTS OF TIME

I was coaching a man who was terribly behind schedule in finishing his dissertation. He hadn't done a thing on the dissertation for several months and was considering abandoning his Ph.D. He agreed to work on the dissertation for

15 minutes, no matter what he felt or thought. He was skeptical that it would work since he had made such small time commitments for daily work before and had never kept them consistently. I suggested that he need only make a commitment to follow this procedure for 1 week. The key to success turned out to be that 1-week commitment. Any time he was tempted to skip his daily 15 minutes, he would remind himself that it was only for a short time. A week did not seem so long to him, but I knew a secret. Inertia tends to keep one going in the direction it is heading. Not working on the dissertation made it more likely that he would not work on the dissertation. Working on it, even a little for a short time, would tend to create more working on the dissertation, which is what happened. He initially made only a 1-week commitment at a time, but soon he no longer needed the commitments to keep himself going. He had made it "over the hump" and, with the end in sight, began to be self-motivated.

This strategy can be used in conjunction with any of the others in this book and this chapter. People are often much more willing and able to put forth effort if their commitment to making that effort is relatively short-lived.

Here's an example from a therapy session:

Client: I'm smoking way too much pot and want to cut back. But each time I tell myself I will smoke less, I don't do it. I still smoke the same amount.

Therapist: Is there anything you really love to do and typically don't do it when you are on pot?

Cl: Yeah. I like to lift weights. I have some in my house. If I smoke dope, I lose all motivation to lift. But when I do lift, I feel really good afterward. It's like it releases endorphins or something. It's not the same as pot, but I get a bit high.

Th: Okay, here's a possibility. For the next two weeks, every time you want to smoke dope, you do 20 minutes of lifting first. Then you can smoke if you want.

Cl: Two weeks. I don't know. I'm not sure.

Th: How about trying it for 1 week and then giving me a call to decide whether you want to commit to another week.

Cl: One week I can do. Sure, that sounds good. You think it'll work?

Th: I don't know. Things like this can or it could just give us more information so we can come up with something else if it doesn't. In any case, you'll probably do a bit more lifting.

Cl: Okay, cool. I'll try it.

CONNECT SMALL STEPS WITH MOTIVATION (POSITIVE OR NEGATIVE)

In my middle years, I began asking the question Paul Simon asks in one of his songs: "Why am I so soft in the middle when the rest of my life is so hard?" I didn't like the midlife paunch I had developed. I wanted to exercise but I wasn't motivated. It was like my early experience with book writing. I didn't like to write. I liked to have written. I liked to have exercised (that is, I wanted the results) but I did not like the process. I had read about the "addiction" regular exercisers get after some time of doing exercise, but I had never experienced such an addiction in previous exercise attempts. So I devised a simple plan to get there. I would pair exercising with something pleasurable. I enjoy the radio interview show *Fresh Air* by Terry Gross and I subscribed to it. I would download the 45-minute show and promised myself I would only listen to it while I was exercising. The show distracted me enough from the initial discomfort that I was able to exercise more easily. And I began slowly. First I did only 15 minutes at a relatively low speed on the treadmill. Then I did 15 minutes but speeded up the treadmill every 5 minutes for 1 minute. Next I begin to increase my time by 5 minutes each week. Now, over a year after I started, I run and walk for 45 minutes (I get to listen to the whole *Fresh Air* show each exercise session—very satisfying) and I've even begun lifting weights a bit. My midlife paunch has almost totally disappeared. The whole thing was so gradual that it was relatively painless.

To recap in the light of the last two chapters: I had a negative motivation (I didn't like my middle getting bigger) and a positive one (I like listening to a radio program). I linked these two motivations with small activities toward my desired future (smaller waistline) and away from my undesired current reality (big belly).

How would this method work in the context of a therapy encounter? Here is an illustrative excerpt:

Client: I am ashamed of this habit I have and I have never told anyone. I pull my hair out when I am nervous. Have you ever heard of this?

Therapist: Yes, I have seen some other people who have pulled their hair out. There is even a name for this—trichotillomania.

Cl: There is. I thought I was the only one who did it. I guess I'm not so much of a freak as I thought.

Th: Everyone has their own unique ways of coping with emotions. You've tried to stop, I assume.

Cl: Yes, many times. I think it is such a habit now that sometimes I don't even know I am doing it. I just find some hair on the floor near me. I don't even remember pulling it out. Other times I am aware of doing it but I just feel I can't stop.

Th: Okay, can you tell me when you would be more likely to pull your hair out and exactly how you do it?

Cl: Well, like I said, it's usually when I am nervous. Like, when I talk to my mother on the phone. She makes me nervous. I pull out my hair almost the whole time I am talking to her. I never do it when anyone else is around and I brush my hair to cover the place where the hair is missing so no one can notice it.

Th: So, you usually pull it out of one spot on your head?

Cl: Yes, but then after a while, I change spots so the hair can grow back on the old place.

Th: And which hand do you usually use to pull the hair out, or is it both hands?

Cl: I've never thought about it, but it is my right hand. I'm right-handed.

Th: And what do you do with your hair after you pull it out?

Cl: Oh my God, this is embarrassing. I didn't know we were going to get into this.

Th: Which part is embarrassing?

Cl: Well, I've gone this far. I might as well be honest. I chew on the root of the hair for a while before I swallow it. God, that is so weird, isn't it?

Th: It doesn't bother me. In fact, it gives me an idea that might help.

Cl: Yeah? Well, I actually feel better having told you. At least someone knows now.

Th: Maybe just having me know will help you change it since it is not so hidden and shameful and you found out you are not alone. I have another idea that might help as well. I would like you to change the pattern a bit. This might seem a little weird, but I would like you to collect the hairs and bring them in to me in a little ziplock bag.

Cl: That would mean I couldn't eat them.

Th: Yes, exactly. That is part of the change. The other part is that you would be letting me in on your formerly shameful, secret habit. What do you think? Are you up for an experiment that might help?

Cl: God, that will be hard, but okay, I'll try it.

Let us give the last word to Charles Handy: "Sometimes, when I consider what tremendous consequences come from little things—a chance word, a tap on the shoulder, or a penny dropped on a newsstand—I am tempted to think there are no little things."

QUESTIONS TO CONSIDER IN USING
THE SMALL-STEPS METHOD OF CHANGE

What is the smallest change you can make in the area you want to change?

What is the shortest time commitment you can make that you think would make a difference and ensure you will stick with the change you agree to try?

What small shift in your focus of attention could you make in the problem situation?

How can you link the small steps you could make with either something you want to avoid or get away from or something you would really like to have or have happen?

THE SMALL-STEPS METHOD OF CHANGE:
A SUMMARY

- Once you find the motivation and energy to change, one way to make that change is to take small steps.
- The first kind of small step is to take small actions or introduce small behavior changes into established problem patterns.

- The next kind of small change is to introduce or foster a small shift in the focus of attention or meanings the person or people have in regard to the problem.

- This method can be effective since it requires only small actions or shifts. The other way to introduce small changes is to suggest making commitments to change for short time periods, rather than permanently or for long periods. Because clients perceive these as more "doable" than longer or bigger shifts, they are more likely to follow through and succeed using this method.

- Link the small change to the motivation the person has.

CHAPTER THREE

The Same Damn Thing:

The Breaking-Patterns Method of Change

Those persons are happiest in this restless and mutable world who are in love with change, who delight in what is new simply because it differs from what is old; who rejoice in every innovation, and find a strange alert pleasure in all that is, and that has never been before. —AGNES REPPLIER

The next method of change, to break up old patterns that one has gotten stuck in or with, was one of Milton Erickson's favorites, and he has provided countless charming and dramatic examples of it in his work.

THE PATTERN VIEW OF LIFE

One of the ways to think about change is to consider problems not as fixed entities—things—but rather as patterns. This view can help foster change by thinking of problems less as set and unchangeable burdens and more as processes. Patterns can be changed at any point in the process. *Things* are much harder to change.

From Milton Erickson (O'Hanlon & Hexum, 1991) I learned a particular approach to changing patterns. First, Erickson emphasized that one must observe the pattern. That means to be like an anthropologist studying and closely observing the elements of the patterns, that is, those elements that repeat without variation. Then, instead of trying to stop the pattern, Erickson suggested, introduce slight changes into it until you find one that breaks the pattern and makes the difference. Introducing small changes into the pattern is like introducing a small crack in the dam and watching the natural force of the water create a bigger and bigger crack until a large change happens.

BREAK THE PATTERN

When cancer researchers are trying to solve the problem of cancer, they don't seem to think about cancer as a thing. They seem to approach it as a process or pattern. There is a genetic component, so some try to intervene by helping identify genes that put people at risk for cancer and then advise high-risk people to get tested regularly. Or perhaps they try to change the expression of the genes that create the conditions for cancer. There is a nutritional element to cancer—certain diets seem to inhibit or encourage the development of cancer. So intervening in diet can block the development of cancer or reduce its likelihood. These researchers do the same thing with proteins, blood supplies to tumors, and so on.

Like them, when I am thinking about change, I am searching for a place in the process where to intervene successfully. I am not particularly concerned about *where* in the process the "right" place for intervention is, as some theoretically committed therapists are. Cognitive therapists prefer to intervene in the beliefs or thinking arena. Behavior therapists focus on the action and environmental aspects of the situation. Feeling-oriented therapists focus on the internal emotional aspects of the problem. Neurologically-oriented psychiatrists hold that giving medications is the most effective approach to changing behavior, cognitive problems, or emotional problems. Almost every approach to change focuses on one area or another and believes this to be the most crucial aspect of the problem (or the solution). But to me it's all process. No one window of intervention is inherently better or more powerful or truer than any other.

My only criteria are: Does it work (that is, help solve the problem) and is it respectful?

There is a case from Milton Erickson (O'Hanlon & Hexum, 1991) that illustrates this principle well. Erickson was working with a man who was very depressed. After working together for some time without the man's depression lifting, Erickson advised him to go to the public library each day and be depressed there instead of at home.

The man dutifully complied but did not really see the point. After some weeks of sitting all day at the library being depressed, he decided to seek some information on a topic in which he had been interested—spelunking (exploring caves). With the help of the librarian, he began reading articles and books on the subject. One day, as he browsed the stacks for a book, another man standing nearby engaged him in a conversation. The man said he had also been interested in exploring caves, but had never done it. He asked the depressed man if he could recommend any good material on the subject. One thing led to another and the two men decided to explore some caves together. This activity and the new friendship gradually began to lift the depression.

When I first heard this story, I used to wonder how Dr. Erickson knew that this would happen. Was he a genius who had anticipated this? After some years and more experience using these kinds of interventions myself, I realized that Erickson could not have known what specifically would happen. But he did know that if the man stayed in his home, very little was likely to change. At least if he were out in a public setting, something new might happen. In his own home sitting alone, there was very little new input, but in public, random changes could happen quite regularly.

I'm sure Dr. Erickson's suggestions did not all lead to the desired results. But on occasion such suggestions do work. Why? Because they break the pattern. Anything that introduces something new into a repeated pattern has the possibility to break the pattern and lead to change. The operative phrase here is "has the possibility." It may not do anything. Or the first several pattern-breaking interventions may not do anything. But one of them might.

This may initially seem exactly the same as the small-steps method of change, but it is different in one crucial way: The small (or large) step taken here is designed to break up a repeating pattern.

Erickson (O'Hanlon & Hexum, 1991) worked with another client who kept putting off her marriage to her fiancé. She had developed a phobia of all forms of trans-portation and her fiancé, in the military in another state, was waiting for her to resolve this problem. After several years, her family brought her to Erickson to see if he could help her. One of the first things he did was to get the young woman to agree to board a public bus by walking backward up the bus steps. She was so embar-rassed by the attention she was calling to herself, she forgot all about her fear.

Yet another of Erickson's (O'Hanlon & Hexum, 1991) cases, strange as it is, illustrates this pattern-breaking method of change. During World War II, Erickson did psychiatric evaluations for the military. The examination usually took only a few minutes, just enough time to assess that there were no major psychiatric problems that would interfere with the soldier doing his job. One young recruit confessed to Erickson that he had a prob-lem that he thought might keep him from serving, but he really wanted to serve. He confessed to Erickson that he could not urinate unless he was urinating through an 8-inch wooden tube. When he was a younger man, he had been caught urinating through the knothole of a fence and had been traumatized by being caught. A few months after being caught, he developed the strange compulsion to urinate through the wooden tube, which he had fashioned himself. He was not able to urinate if he didn't have the tube and he had to carry it everywhere. Erickson told him that if he would cooperate and come to see him every day, he thought they might be able to solve the problem and then Erickson would be able to certify that the young man was psychiatrically fit. The first task Erickson gave the young man was to make a new tube out of bamboo. This slight change was tolerated within the man's compulsion. Next Erickson had him make the tube slightly longer than the previous once. Each day, the young man was instructed to change the length of the tube slightly, sometimes by as little as a sixteenth of an inch. By having the man make it longer, then shorter, then longer then shorter, Erickson eventually had the man being able to urinate through an eighth-inch tube. He casually remarked to the man that holding one's penis while urinating was a bit like holding a tube. Within several days, the man gave up the tube altogether.

I like to use this approach with couples, since they often fall into repetitive and quite nasty patterns of arguing, blaming, and sniping. A couple I was seeing kept getting into trouble because the man would criticize his wife regularly. She would get demoralized. At first she believed his critiques. But later she would think about them and become resentful, as she was pretty sure they were either untrue or were small faults that did not warrant such lengthy critiques.

He agreed that this was a bad habit and one that he wanted to break, but he found it difficult to break it. He agreed to an experiment. He would keep a few helium balloons in the house and when he felt a critique attack coming on, he would inhale the helium and speak in a Mickey Mouse–sounding voice. His wife could no longer take him seriously and would crack up laughing. In the end, they would both end up giggling together. The habit was soon broken.

Another couple used this pattern-breaking method. They would have terrible arguments that would escalate into both of them saying very wounding things they would later regret. When they learned about this idea of breaking the pattern, they came up with their own humorous version of it. If they began to escalate during an argument, they would call for a time-out and head for the bathroom, where the husband would remove all his clothes and lie down in the bathtub. They could continue the argument then, but like the helium couple, they often ended up giggling so much that they couldn't carry on.

An acquaintance of mine read about this pattern-changing method and decided to try it with a persistent and frustrating pattern in her relationship. Her husband had a habit of spending hours lost in used bookstores. He would spend lots of money on this hobby and return home with more books than they had storage for in their home. The time this became the most challenging was when the couple traveled. They had to buy an extra suitcase on many trips just to get the books back home. The husband would say to his wife as they entered the store, "I'll only be an hour or so," but would then go into a bookstore trance in which time would seemingly disappear. They would often spend 4 or 5 hours in the store, with her checking with him regularly and him telling her he was almost finished. This had created many conflicts and had spoiled more than one vacation. She wanted to go to the bookstore with him so they could spend some time together and to try to reduce the time he spent in the store. If unchecked, he might be gone for as long as 8 hours.

After learning about changing patterns, she came up with a plan. They were due to visit relatives in a distant city. A week or so before the trip, she suggested to her husband that since there was a large used bookstore in the city they were to visit, they should plan ahead and bring an extra suitcase. Her husband looked at her with surprise and a little bit of suspicion, but seeing she was serious, he agreed that it was a good idea. When they arrived in the city, she suggested they plan a day to spend at the bookstore. He tried to demure, saying that he would only need to be there for an hour or so. She told him not to worry about it, since this was one of his main pleasures in life. They would go to the bookstore, and she would bring some reading material and entertain herself for as long as he wanted to browse. He was pleasantly surprised at this change of attitude. When they arrived at the bookstore, she settled into a comfortable chair and quickly became absorbed in a novel. Her husband approached her several times, wondering if she needed to go, but she reassured him that she was fine and that he should take as long as he liked. After an hour and a half, he approached her and told her he was ready to go.

This surprised her. She had come up with the plan intending to reduce the conflict between the two of them and to make their trips more pleasant. But her change of the pattern had an unexpected effect. He spent less time in the bookstore. Changing patterns sometimes has this kind of unexpected effect.

There are four simple ways to implement this pattern-breaking method.

1. Change any body behavior associated with the problem pattern.
2. Change the location of the problem pattern.
3. Change the timing or duration of the problem pattern.
4. Change clothing involved in the problem pattern.

Change Any Body Behavior Associated with the Problem Pattern

Example: I have had overeaters eat everything beyond what they are supposed to eat with their nondominant hand. This seems to have the effect of making them aware when they are overeating, as they are often eating unconsciously. It also changes the pattern in a way that can break it.

Change the Location of the Problem Pattern

Example: I have had couples agree to go outside and have their usual argument in the backseat of their car.

Sample therapy dialogue:

Client: I spend hours on the Internet shopping for things. My kids and wife are complaining that I never spend any time with them.

Therapist: Didn't you mention you have wireless Internet access throughout your house?

Cl: Yeah.

Th: How about moving your computer into the kids' playroom and only going online from there?

Cl: That might work. I would still be there with the kids and my wife and they might interrupt my "computer trance" more easily. I can give it a try.

Change the Timing or Duration of the Problem Pattern

Example: I have had people set kitchen timers for 5 minutes during their problem. When the timer goes off, they have to stop the problem pattern for 5 minutes, then continue it for 5 more minutes, and so on. So a person might binge on food for only 5 minutes, rest for 5 or do something else, then binge again for 5 minutes. Or a couple might argue for 5 minutes, rest or go into separate rooms for 5 minutes, then argue for another 5 minutes.

Or if people usually binge in the evening, they agree to binge first thing in the morning.

Sample therapy conversation:

Therapist: It sounds like the arguments get pretty nasty pretty quickly.

Client: Yes.

Th: How about trying an experiment? If things begin to get heated, you take a 15-minute time-out. Set an alarm. Go to separate parts of the house and when you hear the alarm ring, come back together and find out if the mood has changed or if either or both of you have calmed down.

Cl: I am not sure she can do that. She wants to talk about it *now* when she is upset. *I* could do it. I hate these arguments. They don't help me become less upset anyway. I can wait 15 minutes.

Th: Okay, it sounds like at least that's a possibility. Are you both willing to try it?

Cl: Yes.

Change Clothing Involved in the Problem Pattern

A client of mine who would get into bad moods around her periods agreed that when she was feeling PMS [pre-menstrual syndrome] symptoms, she would wear her silliest outfit, some bunny pajamas complete with feet and tail she had received as a joke present for her 30th birthday. She ended up laughing and her family had a warning that she was feeling testy, so they trod carefully during the bunny pjs time.

Another client, who worked from home, found herself avoiding work tasks. She often worked all day in her bathrobe and slippers. She began getting dressed in formal work clothes each morning and was able to get back on track with her work.

Excerpt from a therapy session:

Client: I am so shy and so afraid of making a fool of myself that I never speak up when I have something to say. I feel life just keeps passing me by. I feel like I'll never really live my life.

Therapist: I heard this story once of a woman who was in a similar dilemma and her therapist came up with a creative idea. She suggested that her client rent a clown costume and learn how to do clown makeup and go downtown and hand out balloons and try to make passersby laugh and engage with her. Since she was in disguise, she could hide behind the clown costume and break out of her shell without worrying what people would think of her. Could you do something like that?

Cl: I don't know. It sounds scary but fun in a certain way. I have a friend who works for one of those services that sends people in costume to give birthday greetings and things to people. Maybe I could talk to her and find out what costumes she wears and how it is for her.

Th: It's just an idea. I was just trying to think of something that would get you out of your self-consciousness and a costume seemed like a possibility.

Cl: It might be. I'll have to think about it.

INCREASE OR INTENSIFY THE PATTERN
IN ORDER TO BREAK OR STOP THE PATTERN

This might be considered a fifth way to implement pattern-breaking behavior. For example, a young man at the state hospital compulsively moved his hands up and down all day. Erickson (O'Hanlon & Hexum, 1991) had an aide count the typical number of times the young man moved his hands per minute. It was 125. Erickson then challenged the young man to move faster until his hands were moving 135 times per minute. Then Erickson gradually had the young man reduce the speed until he was moving first 130 times per minute, then 120, then 125, then 115, then 118, then 111, and so on and so forth until he brought the movements down to one or two per minute. The young man eventually stopped moving his hands in any regular fashion.

This was classic Erickson pattern breaking. In another case, he worked with a woman who was constantly going on diets until she reached her "perfect weight," which was 125 pounds. As soon as she got close to 125, she began to weigh herself every few minutes and when the scale finally read 125, she would compulsively eat and gain back all she had lost on the diet. The same pattern had happened for years and she was desperate, she told Erickson, to stop the yo-yo cycle and stabilize her weight. Erickson found out that the most the woman had ever weighed was 180, which she weighed at the time she sought his help. He got her to agree to gain between $2\,{}^1\!/_2$ and 5 pounds more before she could lose weight. She was to check her weight compulsively until she gained the required weight. She reported back after she had gained the $2\,{}^1\!/_2$ pounds and begged Erickson to let her begin losing weight, but he told her the agreement was for her to gain between $2\,{}^1\!/_2$ and 5 pounds. She dutifully went home and gained exactly $3\,{}^3\!/_4$ pounds. Then Erickson let her begin her weight loss. She hit 125 without the usual compulsive weighing pattern and never regained the weight.

Th: About the panic attacks, I have something that might work.

Cl: What?

Th: Well, part of panic attacks involves being afraid of being panicked, so I think there are a couple of ways to decrease the severity or frequency of the attacks by eliminating at least the fear of having them. It involves planning and deliberately bringing on a panic attack or some part of it. For example, if you start to feel one coming on, you could try to bring one on deliberately rather than trying to avoid or stop it. Pick a good place to faint, one that is soft and won't result in any injuries, and tell yourself that that would be a great place to faint.

Cl: [*laughs*] Well, that would be different.

Th: Yeah. You would be in control rather than out of control. It's a bit like falling into quicksand. The more you struggle, the quicker you sink. If you relax at bit more and stop struggling, there is a possibility of getting out of the quicksand.

Cl: That makes sense. The medications aren't really helping that much and I spend most of my time trying to make sure I don't get panicked.

Th: You could also try to put yourself in situations that would bring on panic, but again, do it very deliberately. Take back a bit of your life by bringing on the fear you usually avoid.

Cl: That might be harder. But I could try to make the panic come when I feel it starting. That seems more doable to me.

Th: Okay.

LINK THE PROBLEM PATTERN TO SOMETHING ELSE

Each time the problem begins to occur, link another element to it.

I treated a woman who was bingeing and vomiting. I found out she had a favorite pair of shoes and asked her to stop whatever she was doing when she was about to binge and put on her favorite shoes. She complied with the request and found that, often, it helped her stop the binge. She explained that putting on the shoes somehow gave her a brief moment of awareness of what she was doing and also reminded her that she was currently in therapy to stop this pattern. Previously, she would go on automatic pilot during her bulimic episodes.

Erickson (O'Hanlon & Hexum, 1991) had a patient who began to have panic attacks before he had to appear as an anchorman on the nightly news. He convinced the man that he suffered from an excess of energy that was coming out through the panic attacks. The assignment Erickson gave the man was to do 50 deep knee bends as rapidly as possible before he went on the air to stave off the panic attacks, giving himself enough time to catch his breath before the broadcast began. The intervention worked and the panics disappeared.

Sample dialogue from a clinical setting:

> Therapist: Each time you avoid doing your taxes or paying your bills, you agree to do 50 sit-ups. It doesn't matter if you do them all at once or over the course of the hour, as long as you do them before you do anything else.
>
> Client: I'll either start handling things or I'll have the flattest stomach in town.
>
> Th: Yep. You win either way.

FIND, HIGHLIGHT, AND EXPAND SOLUTION PATTERNS

Dr. Erickson (O'Hanlon & Hexum, 1991) used to pick his son up from school. One day, his son and his son's friend, Jake, were particularly quiet when they got in the car.

Erickson asked the boys what was wrong. Jake looked at the floor and remained silent. Erickson's son, after an awkward silence, reported that Jake had been humiliated by the teacher just before class had ended. She held up his rather messy paper for the entire class to see and berated Jake for having such poor handwriting. None of the words were on the line, she complained. The letters were virtually unreadable. Erickson asked to see Jake's paper and he reluctantly handed it over. Erickson looked over the paper and, indeed, it was a mess. But before he handed it back to Jake, he commented, "That *t* is certainly on the line."

Every day after school, Erickson would ask to see Jake's paper from that day. The second day, Erickson said, "That *t* and that *h* are both on the line and there is good spacing between them." By the third week, there was more and more for Erickson to compliment Jake about. His handwriting was improving. By the end of the year, Jake had won the class award for the most improvement over the course of the year and was feeling very proud of himself.

This example illustrates a simple pattern-changing method: noticing aspects of the problem situation that are not problems and amplifying them.

Import Patterns of Competence From Another Setting and Substitute Them for the Problem Pattern

When Erickson (O'Hanlon & Hexum, 1991) was in college, he didn't have much money. He found what seemed like the ideal boarding room situation. He would get a substantial break on his room and board at the boardinghouse if he would agree to teach the owner of the boardinghouse to read. "Ma," as the proprietor of the boardinghouse was known to all, had grown up in a family in which her father had thought it a waste of time to teach females to read, since they were going to be farmwives and wouldn't need such an unnecessary skill. By the time she had married, she found she had a block to learning to read and write, even though her husband tried to teach her and was supportive of her efforts to master these abilities. Through the years, after her children were born and had learned to read and write, they all tried to teach Ma but did not succeed. She and her husband had finally sold their farm and moved into town.

After her husband died, Ma began to rent out her house to students at the local college. Through the ensuing years, she made it known that if someone would teach her to read and write, she would give them a break on rent. No one had succeeded until Erickson arrived. He took a different tack. After hearing about how all the others had failed and about Ma's block, he told her that he wanted to start by having her learn to be comfortable just holding a pencil and making marks. He had her make random marks: straight lines, jagged lines, circles, dots, and so on all over the paper. She did this for a week or so. Then Erickson reminded her of her years on the farm (he had also grown up on a farm). He told her she was not to try to read or write yet, but that he wanted her to begin to draw common objects from the farm. Draw an A-frame roof. She could do that with no problem. Draw a tire. Again, no problem. Draw a rake leaning against the side of a barn. Draw two doughnuts. Draw a doughnut with a bite taken out of it. Draw a formation of geese flying in the sky. Now lay a board across the A-frame roof right in the middle.

Soon, Erickson had guided Ma in making the shapes of each of the letters. He did not inform her that she was writing, so as not to trigger her block. But he reminded her of how each animal on the farm had a name. There was Bessie the cow and Henry the horse and so on. Each of these shapes had a name and she was to learn each of the names. After getting her to put the shapes of the letters in alphabetical order, he began to teach her the names. She had a good memory, having had to use it quite a bit through her life since she could not jot things down to remember them. She proudly memorized each of the names of the figures she had drawn. Then Erickson had her put letters together and had her memorize the names of the groups of letters. She did well at this. One day, Erickson had her put together words to make this sentence, which was a favorite phrase her deceased husband used often: Get going, Ma, and fix me some grub. When she read this aloud, Erickson told her that this was reading. She broke down in tears when the realization finally hit her. She took great pride in reading letters she received from her children and reading the

Bible and she progressed rapidly in her studies, with no further problems with her block.

This example illustrates the method of finding competence patterns from another context and transferring them to the problem context to help solve the problem. Here are a few more.

I was working with an engineer and his wife. She was unhappy about how unexpressive he was and about some other problems in the marriage. He had previously responded to her complaints by telling her that she was irrational and too sensitive and emotional. This did not go over well with her and she was considering getting a divorce. I gave him the task of debugging his marital system, identifying places where the system broke down, and brainstorming about possible fixes for the glitches. He returned to the next session with a flow chart diagramming typical problems and possible solutions. He was very enthusiastic about this and his wife was impressed that he had put so much time and effort into it. In the third session, his wife and I helped him identify the specifications for a good hug. It had to be at least 45 seconds in duration, full frontal contact, and no talking. He was to wait for her to begin to pull away before he let go. He again took to this approach well and was eager for more specifications. Once we found a way to use his rationality and analytical mind, things moved rapidly in a positive direction and his wife gave up her plans for splitting up the marriage.

When I was teaching a workshop with Michele Weiner-Davis (1988, personal communication), she told the story of a woman in her 30s who was lamenting the fact that she could not find a relationship. Michele knew that the woman was a highly successful sales and marketing executive and asked the woman how she would go about designing a sales and marketing campaign for finding the right mate. The woman's attitude went from discouraged and complaining to energized within a short time. When she returned in a subsequent session, she had already begun to implement her plan and it was showing preliminary results.

When I was on *Oprah* talking about the ideas in my book *Do One Thing Different* (O'Hanlon, 2000) she showed a video of a woman who had tried the do-one-thing-different method of change. She said she had always suffered from low self-esteem. She was constantly hiding her face beneath her hair, slumping down, and avoiding eye contact with people. Some years earlier, she had been fascinated to observe the same pattern with England's Prince Charles's new fiancé, Diana. In early press conferences, Diana seemed painfully shy and awkward, hiding her face beneath her hair, mumbling her replies to queries, looking down, and so on. But through the years, Diana had blossomed into a self-confident person who stood up straight and looked world leaders, children, reporters, AIDS victims, and others in the eye. The woman on the *Oprah* video had decided that for her one-thing-different experiment, she would try acting like the latter-day Diana for 1 week. She was amazed at the changes she experienced. Although all she did was stand up straight and begin to make eye contact, people at work began asking her whether she had had a makeover. Men began rushing to open doors for her as they never had before. More than that, after some days, she actually began to feel better about herself.

Here's how this might go in a therapy session:

Client: There's this girl at school that I like but I am too afraid to ask her out.

Therapist: Is there anything else that you have done that was really hard for you but you did it?

Cl: At summer camp, we did this thing where we rappelled down a cliff. Boy, that was scary, but I did it.

Th: How did you get yourself to do it even though it was so scary?

Cl: There were other people who were there telling me to go for it. And finally I just jumped out and did it. It wasn't really that bad once I was over the edge. Thinking about it was more scary than doing it.

Th: How about using the same strategy for asking this girl out. Get some encouragement from others and then just make the leap.

Cl: I never thought of it like that. I think that would work.

STOP THE PATTERN: JUST DON'T DO IT!

I read a story some time ago about a man who had tried everything to lose weight. And indeed he did manage to lose weight at times, only to gain it back (and sometimes more) later. Finally, in desperation, he decided no expert, diet, book, or program could help him. He had a sense he had to discover and confront what was driving his overeating. One weekend, he was ready for his task. He ate a healthy, normal breakfast. A relatively short time later, he noticed he was feeling hungry. He knew from experience that this wasn't actual calorie hunger, but was more an emotional signal. Instead of eating, which he had done in the past when he felt hungry, he was determined to find out what lay beneath these emotional hunger signals. He sat on his couch and waited. Soon he noticed the stirrings of fear. He was afraid of something nameless. The fear began to grow, but still he did not give in to the urge to eat. The fear grew and grew until it became a full-blown terror. His body began to shake and he began to sweat. He had never felt such fear in his life, but he was determined to ride it through and find out what was at its bottom. After several hours of shaking and sweating, the fear began to subside. He never did determine what it was he was afraid about. It was just a feeling of fear and terror. He repeated this procedure every time he felt the emotional hunger signal through-out the weekend. Gradually, the fear diminished in both intensity and duration until it was lasting only 5 minutes or so per episode. When the weekend was over and he returned to work, he would take short breaks and go into the restroom to shake and sweat until the fear subsided. Gradually, the emotional hunger and fear disappeared and he permanently lost the weight.

These days this is called mindfulness, which is derived from a Buddhist meditation practice of noticing only one's thoughts, feelings, and experience. In this practice, one does not react or judge or try to change anything, but merely to become aware of feelings, thoughts, sensations, and behavior. This can be a major pattern change since most of the time when we have problems we are doing something to change those problems. In our "fix-it" culture, doing nothing may be a profound change.

Again, here's how it might go in a session:

Therapist: The next time you have the urge to binge, I would like you to try and experiment. Just observe the feelings and thoughts you have for about 10 minutes without acting on any of them. Notice where the feelings or sensations are occurring in your body. Notice any voice tones or qualities associated with your thoughts, if there are any. Notice which thoughts repeat, if any. Notice anything else, without doing anything to change them or to act on them. If after the 10 minutes, you still decide to binge, you can go ahead. If you decide at that point that you no longer need to binge of course, you can skip it.

LIFE KARMA: CHALLENGING AND CHANGING BROADER PATTERNS

So far the examples I have given deal with changing specific problems, but there is a broader way to make change. People sometimes have problem patterns that repeat over time and repeat in multiple contexts and relationships. I call these broader patterns life karma. They can be patterns like avoidance or running away from difficult situations. They might be patterns like selecting spouses who are very much reminiscent of one of your parents. They might be patterns like being impulsive. Or patterns like worry and anxiety. Or shyness. Or self-criticism. Or it might be a conviction that we are destined to never have enough money.

These patterns rest on beliefs or premises and are supported by actions and interactions. We might gravitate to a certain person or situation because that person or situation reflects a premise or nonconscious idea or belief we have. We might believe that we don't deserve happiness or love. Or we might be very wary of, but inadvertently inviting, criticism.

Here's the way one of these life karma patterns might work. If you were afraid or concerned about being criticized, you might start to withhold information from your partner or friends that you think they might critique you about. Then, when they find out the withheld information at some later time, they would probably critique you for being dishonest or a coward. The belief or premise ("I may be criticized and I couldn't take that") would be supported by the behavior or interaction.

Therefore, to challenge one of these life karma patterns, find some cornerstone that supports the whole thing. It might be the underlying belief or premise. You

could begin to be aware of when that premise is func-
tioning in your life. I sometimes say that these thoughts
are different from other thoughts. These are the thoughts
that think us rather than the thoughts we think. You
could challenge the thoughts. "It is okay to be criticized.
I have been criticized before and have survived." Or you
might challenge the actions or interactions. "Even though
I am afraid to be critiqued, I know that withholding
information is not the best solution. I am going to be
forthright even if it leads to my being criticized."

If your belief or premise is that you will never have
enough money, you might challenge this belief by sav-
ing enough money so that you will feel secure no matter
what happens (that is intervening at the level of action).
Or you might try doing some of those reprogramming
methods like affirmations. You might educate yourself
about money or apprentice yourself to a mentor who can
model or teach you another way of thinking or acting.

Joe had damaged each of his three long-term relationships by having sexual affairs. In his current relationship, Joe's partner, who had known about his
previous affairs, had decided to give him a chance to
change this pattern. Joe and I discussed his entire life.
He was sexually abused when he was a child and was
raised in a family and religion that held a view that sex
was shameful. His sexuality "went underground," as he
said it. He had tried to resolve this by exploring sex in
various ways and had thought he had put these patterns
behind him until his recent affair. In discussing it, the

pattern that went through his entire life was secret masturbation. Even when having good and frequent sex with his partner, Joe would sneak off and masturbate without telling her. His current partner had known of this pattern and had told Joe that there was nothing to be ashamed about in masturbating, so he could feel free to tell her instead of hiding it. At first, this had seemed liberating. But at one period in the relationship, Joe had felt guilty because he began to prefer masturbating to having sex with his partner. She had begun to complain about the lack of sex and Joe had begun to hide his masturbation again. During masturbation, he began to fantasize about a woman at work. Gradually this led him to begin flirting with the woman at work and then to the affair.

Joe decided to experiment with stopping masturbation. It had never occurred to him to try this before because it seemed to him that this was going backward into shame again. When we discussed changing life karma, Joe thought that this was a pivotal behavior in his cheating. He initially made a commitment to stop for a month. This was challenging since it had been a daily habit, but Joe began to feel less and less compulsive. He extended the commitment to a year. With some other work, his marriage began to heal from the affair.

Karin had always been attracted to devilishly handsome "bad boys," and the relationships had always ended badly. She met a man, Jim, casually through a friend and he asked her out, but she was not interested because he wasn't "her type." After another relationship with "her type" went sour, though, she called up her friend and asked for Jim's number. She and Jim went out for a date and she still thought that nothing would come out of it because she had not been attracted to him. She liked Jim, though. He was smart and had a good sense of humor. Jim liked Karin a lot and was willing to be patient. They continued to date casually and after about 6 months, Karin was surprised to find herself being more and more attracted to Jim. They eventually married. Karin likes to joke with her single friends who are complaining about not being able to find a good man like Jim that they should try going out with someone who is not their type.

Here's an excerpt from a therapy conversation:

> Client: It seems I always get involved with guys who are afraid of committing 100%. I am involved with this guy right now who has a girlfriend. He keeps trying to decide between me and her. He hasn't told her about me but I know about her. But this is only the latest in a string of relationships that only seem to go so far. It is uncanny.

> Therapist: If you had an unconscious motive or deep idea about yourself, life, or relationships that this pattern reflected, what do you think it might be?

> Cl: I don't know. I've been thinking it's men for many years, but friends of mine seem to be able to find guys who are willing to commit. Maybe it is something I am creating.

> Th: I am not sure I would think about it as creating, but maybe you have some hand in it and that's the

part you have control over and could potentially change. I've heard this pattern form in a few other people over the years I've been a therapist, and one of the common themes that connected those other situations is that the people deep down didn't think they deserved love or to be happy. Another theme is that relationships always break up, so find men who are ambivalent. Then your whole heart isn't at risk, since you know it's not safe to give your heart to an ambivalent person. But it might be something else in your situation. Does either of those ring true or can you think of something else it might be?

Cl: I've always had the idea that I have good self-esteem, but lately I've been thinking that that might just be on the surface and deep down I don't like myself very much. I am pretty critical of myself really. Perhaps it's that I don't think I am worthy of a good man or good relationship.

Th: It might be. One way to investigate that would be to ask yourself: What would a person who really felt good about herself do in your current situation? Would she stay in or end the relationship or have a serious talk with her boyfriend? If one of your friends who is involved with a committed guy gave you advice, what do you think she would say?

Cl: I'm sure a person with high self-esteem wouldn't have stayed this long. Deep down I don't think he is ever going to commit to me.

Th: What would you do in this situation that would be unlike you but consistent with a person who did think she is worthy?

Cl: I am not sure, but I am going to think about it in that way. It's a new way of thinking about it and I have a sense it will lead me somewhere.

GUIDELINES FOR CHANGING PERSISTENT UNHELPFUL LIFE PATTERNS

1. Notice results you don't like that recur.

   Examples:

   Always being in debt

   Harmful addictive or compulsive behaviors, such as overdrinking, unsafe and inappropriate sexual activities, overeating, overworking, and so on

   Arguments or conflicts in intimate relationships

   Being regularly taken advantage of by people

   Accommodating to others in a way that compromises your integrity or well-being

2. Investigate and notice your actions, feelings, and underlying ideas or thoughts in these recurring problematic situations.

   If you can, identify what outcome or feeling you are trying to prevent or avoid by reacting or acting the way you do. Often, our attempted solutions to some problem become the problem.

Examples:

You are afraid you will be controlled.

You blame the other person so you won't be blamed.

You leave first so you won't be left or rejected or abandoned.

You eat so you won't feel so lonely or sad or frightened.

You shop to distract yourself from an unhappy relationship or situation.

Hint: If you are having trouble identifying any of these elements, ask for help from a trusted friend, a loving partner, or an insightful therapist/coach.

3. Do something different from your usual actions, reactions, or patterns

Possible strategies:

Just notice the impulse to act or react.

Just notice and stay with the feeling you were trying to avoid.

Do something that might actually invite the avoided feeling.

Stay in a situation that you would normally leave because you were trying to avoid discomfort.

Write out or tell someone about the feeling, fear, or outcome you were trying to avoid or forestall.

4. Repeat until you break the automatic pattern or stop getting the unwanted results

Examples:

You get out of debt and stay out of debt.

You stop having the same old argument or conflict in this or any relationship.

You stay in a relationship beyond the point you would have withdrawn or left.

You stop drinking or stop drinking in a way that messes up your life.

QUESTIONS TO ASK REGARDING THE CHANGING-PATTERNS METHOD OF CHANGE

What are some repeating results in your life or relationships that you are unhappy with or frustrated by?

What is the smallest change you could make in your problem situation that you think might make a difference?

Where in the problem situation do you keep repeating some pattern of action you could change?

Is there anywhere you have some competence that you could draw upon to solve this problem? What patterns could you import from this area of competence to substitute for the problem patterns or begin to find your way out of the problem pattern?

Can you think of something absurd you could do that would shake everything up in the problem situation?

What are your typical automatic interpretations?

What do you think or believe you must do or be or have?

What do you think or believe you cannot do or be or have?

What do you believe is the nature of people, the world, life, and relationships?

What is something that someone with a belief like yours would never do?

What is one action you could take that would be incompatible with a premise you have been living with?

How can you come up with a plan to notice and interrupt your automatic reaction or interpretation in some situation in which one of your premises has dominated?

BREAKING-PATTERNS METHOD OF CHANGE: A SUMMARY

- First, identify a pattern related to the problem you and the client have identified.

  ◦ Usually it is important to get a good sensory-based description of the pattern involving actions and observations, not theories and explanations.

  ◦ If you can't specify the pattern in what can be observed, find some internal patterns like a series of inner pictures or repetitive, internal self-talk.

- Next, together with your clients, find some place in the pattern to interrupt it, add something new, or divert it into a new direction.

  ◦ Find some actions that clients can change and will agree to change.

∘ Or find some shift in the internal pattern that clients are willing and able to make. This is usually more challenging than making changes in actions.

• Get clients to commit to trying the pattern change as an experiment, for whatever period of time is workable and you and they think will be enough time to find out whether the change makes a positive difference.

• Check back with clients in subsequent sessions or by phone to find out what happened. Frame the pattern change as an experiment so there is no right or wrong response, just information.

• If they didn't follow through on their agreement to make the change, find out what got in the way. You might need to ratchet the level of energy, the amount of time, the length of time, or the action or change involved to make it more likely to be followed through. Don't immediately assume resistance.

• If, after adjustments, clients still don't follow through on their commitment, then question them about their motivation and make certain you have linked the pattern change to the motivation.

• If clients follow through and it doesn't result in a change that is positive and significant or lasting, then try some other pattern changes or try another of the change methods listed in this book.

CHAPTER FOUR

52-Card Pickup:

The Crisis Method of Change

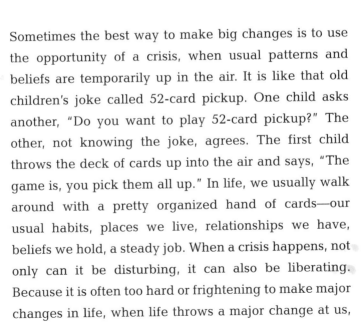

Turbulence is life force. It is opportunity. Let's love turbulence and use it for change. —RAMSAY CLARK

Sometimes the best way to make big changes is to use the opportunity of a crisis, when usual patterns and beliefs are temporarily up in the air. It is like that old children's joke called 52-card pickup. One child asks another, "Do you want to play 52-card pickup?" The other, not knowing the joke, agrees. The first child throws the deck of cards up into the air and says, "The game is, you pick them all up." In life, we usually walk around with a pretty organized hand of cards—our usual habits, places we live, relationships we have, beliefs we hold, a steady job. When a crisis happens, not only can it be disturbing, it can also be liberating. Because it is often too hard or frightening to make major changes in life, when life throws a major change at us, we might be able to use that up-in-the-air moment to question and change something. This is not to minimize the pain involved in going through or experiencing life crises, but merely to suggest that since the pain and crisis might be inevitable, there may be a way to extract some value from them in addition to the trauma.

There is some research (Dabrowski, 1964; McMillen, 1999; McMillen, Curtis, & Fisher, 1998) that shows that, counter to the prevailing notion most of us have these days that stress or crises inevitably result in posttraumatic stress problems, at times stress can lead to positive growth.

THE THREE Cs

The simplest "formula" I can give for turning crisis into growth or posttraumatic stress into posttraumatic success is this: use the 3 Cs: connection, compassion, and contribution. I have written about these three elements in several of my previous books (O'Hanlon, 2003, 2006).

The research in this area and my own observations show that if one can make deeper and better connections with oneself, others, and some bigger sense of things or meanings after a crisis, one can thrive or grow as a result of the crisis. We know from the field of trauma studies that disconnection is often the result of trauma or crises. People disconnect from their bodies, memories, or experience. They disconnect from their social connections and withdraw from the world. And their sense of meaning is often shattered. They blame God or lose faith. Their assumptions about what life means and whether it is safe to trust the world or life are challenged.

Connection

My sister-in-law was in a bad accident and was in the hospital. I spoke to my brother during her recovery and told him about the research I was finding about the potential positive outcomes of crises and tragedy. He told me that he and his wife had just been talking about that the night before. My sister-in-law had been a stay-at-home mom for many years, then worked as a secretary at the local school. She never had the sense that her life had been that important, but the amount of flowers that showed up in her hospital room had frankly shocked her into seeing how much she meant to so many people. She felt connected to her social support network in a way she never would have if the accident had not happened. She had also told my brother that being laid up in a hospital bed for so long had made her appreciate her body and health in a way that she never had. She vowed to him and to herself that she would lose some weight and get into shape when she recovered. She had connected to her body in a new way as a result of the accident. Their marriage also developed a stronger connection due to the realization that they could have lost each other.

Compassion

Rudy Guiliani, former mayor of New York City, was widely seen as a harsh, law-and-order leader. He became unpopular with many during his tenure. Then the terrorists attacked the World Trade Center towers. In his last few months in office—the months after the attacks—he became one of the most beloved and admired figures in the city, as well as in the country. When he was interviewed some years later by popular talk show host Oprah Winfrey, a video of him crying with survivors and victims' families was shown. He attended countless funerals and baptisms and weddings of the victims and their families and was openly emo- tional during these ceremonies. When Winfrey asked him about this seeming change of character, he spoke about having had cancer a few years previously. Guil- iani said, "The point of biggest change . . . was prostate cancer. It helped me a lot. . . . It turned out to be very fortunate that I was diagnosed with prostate cancer in that it made me grow a lot as a person. . . . It was a gift. . . . It made me a deeper person. You go through a traumatic experience like that and you either recede as a person or you grow. I think prostate cancer and going through September 11th were things that helped me to grow" (2002).

We have seen other public figures who have gone through public scandals and humiliations (notably Rush Limbaugh, who was accused of buying illegal pain medications, and Bill O'Reilly, who was accused of sexual harassment) who did not seem to soften or develop more compassion as a result of their crises. I predict more posttraumatic problems for such people.

Contribution

Candy Lightener's daughter was killed by a repeat drunk driver. Instead of giving up or becoming bitter, Lightener dedicated her life to reducing and stopping drunk driving accidents and deaths. She founded Mothers Against Drunk Driving (M.A.D.D.). Adam Walsh was kidnapped and killed as a child. His father, John Walsh, became a well-known crusader against crime, hosting a television show that has led to the capture of many criminal fugitives. Nelson Mandela took his 27 years of torture and imprisonment and decided to use the experience to help lead his country, South Africa, from the hatred of apartheid and the possibility of bloody reprisals into an integrated, peaceful society. All these people used crisis to move them to make contributions out of the pain of their ordeals. If one seeks to wound others or withdraw from society, one cannot so readily get the value from the crisis or trauma.

Using the 3 Cs to Turn Trauma and Crises into Growth and Positive Change

Turn disconnection into deeper and better connections
Turn harshness into compassion
Turn pain into contribution

WAKE-UP CALLS

Crises can also serve as wake-up calls. Many people tend to live life by inertia. You will continue on the path you are on, usually set by your family of origin, your culture, and early decisions unless something gets you to reexamine the direction you are taking. Crises can give you the time and opportunity to change course or recommit to an earlier abandoned dream. Leslie Lebeau wrote, "It often takes a crisis to break through our usual models of the world. A crisis is a gift, an opportunity, and perhaps a manifestation that life loves us, by beckoning us to go beyond the dance we presently perform" (quoted in Andreas, 1996). Crises can be opportunities for deep truth-telling and soul-searching.

Charles Darwin developed many of his main ideas about evolution while he was laid up in bed with a serious illness.

Actress Debra Winger was on her way to becoming a sociologist like her brother when she fell off a ride at the amusement park where she worked. She broke her skull open and required serious surgery. During her recovery, she thought about her life and decided she wanted to do something important; sociology would not cut it. She decided at that time to become an actress and she did, with enough skill and passion to ultimately be nominated for several Oscars.

Poet David Whyte (1999) told a story in his lectures of meeting a well-known landscape architect in Great Britain about the time Whyte was trying to decide what to do with his life. This man was obviously very successful and well established and seemed to love his work, which involved designing large parks all over the UK. The man said the story was a little unusual, but the truth of it was that he had been a drug addict in his younger years. He was living a quite squalid life, illegally squatting in a house in London with other addicts. One day he decided that his life was going nowhere and he became determined to kill himself. He attempted to throw himself from an upper-story window. But he was so disabled by the drugs he was taking that his sweater got caught on a nail on the window ledge and he was slammed face-first into a window box filled with dirt and dead plants just outside the window. He couldn't even free himself from the nail, so impaired was he. As he lay there, face pressed into the dirt, he began to cry, pitying himself and his desperate situation. Just then, when he thought things couldn't get any worse, it began to rain. But he was stuck. As he lay there, he became fascinated with the rivulets and patterns that the rain was creating in the window box. Hours later, when he was finally sober enough to free himself, he had a newfound conviction that he would learn landscaping.

Writer John Lescroart had been published but wasn't a full-time writer when he had a crisis that called him to make a greater commitment to his writing. One day in 1989, when he was 41, he went bodysurfing. The next day found him in a hospital with spinal meningitis, which he had contracted while in the ocean. Doctors thought he had only 2 hours to live. He battled death for 11 days, and when he finally emerged, he decided to quit his day job and devote himself fully to writing. He has made a living as a writer ever since and his books are now routinely best sellers.

In my early years, I had the idea that major crises were rare in life and that they needed to be resolved quickly to prevent the damage that trauma can cause. Having had several of my own "good breakdowns," however, and having observed many others in clients and friends, I have come to the conclusion that major crises are more common than I had supposed and that crises may be life's way of getting us to shed our old, too-small skin and grow into the next phases of our lives.

Here's a clinical example

> Therapist: Getting fired sounds like it really did a number on you. Now you're here, you've gotten yourself out of bed and out of the house, so in some ways you seem like you're bouncing back, at least a little. Let me ask you about how you coped with this setback. Did this crisis lead to you connecting with other people in a new or better way at all or did it lead to more isolation for you?

> Client: Well, I became a lot closer to my sister, who has really been there for me. But I think I lost touch with some friends, especially the ones from work. They called me but I never called them back. I was just too bummed out.

> Th: And do you think this crisis time has made you think about your life in a different way or gotten you to decide to change any parts of your life that weren't working or weren't right in some way?

Cl: Yeah, I have decided never to put all my eggs in one basket again. I think I want to get another job to help get back on my feet financially, but I also have this idea for my own business and I plan to work on that part-time until I can build it up more and then quit that job to work for myself. I also realized I didn't really like doing programming even though I am good at it. I would rather do something like build Web sites, which involves a lot more contact with people and also graphic design, which I want to learn more about. I have been thinking about starting a Web site for people who have been downsized or fired that can help get them through better than I have gotten through. You know, not to make money or anything from the site, just to help people.

Th: That sounds good. By helping others you might even get some good tips yourself for getting another job or moving through this time a bit faster.

Cl: Yeah, I was thinking that. I could find the best sites for job seekers and sites for dealing with depression and put up links to those.

QUESTIONS FOR USING THE CRISIS METHOD OF CHANGE

What crises have you had that have helped you make positive changes?

How could you use this time of crisis to make deeper and better connections to yourself and others?

How can you use this crisis or trauma to become
   more compassionate toward yourself and others?

How has this crisis made you more sensitive to the
   suffering of others?

How can you find a way to make a contribution to
   others or the world out of the experience of your
   crisis or trauma?

How can you use this crisis or trauma as a wake-up
   call, that is, an opportunity to tell some avoided
   truth or to take a new direction in your life?

CRISIS METHOD OF CHANGE: A SUMMARY

• Investigate how major life crises have led to:

  ◦ **Connection:** How has a crisis or trauma led to better or
    deeper connections to yourself, others, or the bigger
    picture or meaning?

  ◦ **Compassion:** How has a crisis or trauma led you
    to soften or accept yourself and/or others?

  ◦ **Contribution:** How has the crisis or truama led
    to finding ways to help others who have been
    through similar troubles?

  ◦ **Wake-Up Calls:** How has the crisis reawakened
    earlier or forgotten dreams? How has the crisis led
    to a change in life direction? How has the crisis
    helped you to realize where and how you were off
    track in your life, relationships, or careers?

CHAPTER FIVE

Bless My Soul:
The Mentor/Model Method of Change

We are each of us angels with only one wing, and we can only fly by embracing each other. —LUCIANO DE CRESCENZO

One of the ways people change is to be inspired by mentors or role models. Sometimes we model people from afar. At other times they become our direct mentors and supporters. Sometimes they become negative mentors or role models, showing us what we don't want to become or representing someone whose negative pronouncements we work to disprove.

NEGATIVE MENTORS AND ROLE MODELS

When I first realized that I was going to write books and begin giving workshops, I did not have much of an idea about how to proceed. I spoke to an older colleague who had one book published and was teaching workshops.

We had both studied with Milton Erickson. I thought he might have some guidance and advice for me and indeed he did. "You'll never get a book published with just a master's degree, Bill. You need a Ph.D. or an M.D. to get published. These are the only degrees that will give you credibility." I was a bit stunned. I was ready to write and teach *now*. I didn't plan to go back to school.

After recovering from the initial shock, I thought it through. He wasn't right, I thought. Jay Haley, another of Erickson's students, had published many books and he, like me, had a master's degree. He taught workshops and had made a significant contribution to the field of therapy. So I decided to proceed as if what I wanted to do was possible. Some 1,500 public speaking engagements and 24 books later, I guess my colleague was wrong.

Erickson (O'Hanlon & Hexum, 1991) had a similar experience. When he had polio at the age of 17, his local doctor sent for three specialists from the big city to confirm the diagnosis. They arrived, examined Erickson in his fevered state, and stepped just outside the bedroom. Erickson overheard them telling his mother, "The boy won't last the night." Hearing his mother so upset and the casual way these doctors made this announcement to her made Erickson mad; he vowed to prove those damn city slicker doctors wrong.

He was feverish through the night and almost died several times, but when dawn broke he insisted that his family move the dresser near his bed so that he could watch the sunrise in the mirror atop the dresser. They thought he was hallucinating, but complied with his urgent request. He fell asleep with a smile on his face.

When he awoke, he was paralyzed. The three city doctors returned and he heard them tell his family, "Well, he survived the fever, but he will never walk again." How do you think Erickson responded to this prediction? Of course, as you might imagine, he became determined to walk again one day. It took him some time, but he did finally walk again, against all odds.

POSITIVE MENTORS AND BLESSINGS

There are people who directly encourage us along the way. They can help us change and go further in our lives and careers than we ever imagined we could. I found a quotation from Kenny Ausubel: "Each of us has a spark of life inside us, and our highest endeavor ought to be to set off that spark in one another." Those people who spark us off are mentors and people who bless us.

Early in my career, when I was more a legend in my own mind than well known in my chosen field, I became friends with psychologist Stephen Gilligan, another of Erickson's students and protégés. We would make a point of meeting for a meal when we were at the same international conferences. Steve would ask me what I was up to and I would answer with my usually enthusiastic recounting of all my plans ("I am writing three books and I have come up with this exciting idea called solution-oriented therapy."). I am a little hyper and Steve is preternaturally calm. He would wait until I stopped bouncing in the restaurant booth, look me deeply in the eye, and intone, "Bill, I think you are up to something big." I would feel an electric energy surge through my body and soul. "Steve sees it," I would think. "Maybe it will happen. Maybe I do have something big to contribute to the field. Perhaps I'm not just fooling myself." That belief and support kept me going through the early years of my career. I felt I had been given a blessing.

Perhaps you were blessed by a parent who told you you could do anything you set your mind to. Perhaps you were blessed by a teacher who believed in your goodness.

Psychologist Patrick Carnes (1990), well known for his original work in the area of sexual addiction, grew up in a troubled household where there wasn't much support. Patrick escaped from this painful environment by reading books. His grade-school librarian noticed his interest and began to steer him to books she thought he would like. Coincidentally, or perhaps by design, she transferred to the high school he attended the year he began there, so they had a mentoring relationship for 4 more years. Carnes felt that the reason he attended college was due to this librarian. He attributed at least part of his recovery from his own addictions to her support and belief in him in his crucial early years, when he most needed such support.

Mentors not only can see potential in us and bless us, but they can also offer specific help and guidance at crucial times in our lives and careers.

I heard a story about a young woman, Jane, who grew up during the turbulent 1960s. She, like many young people, experimented with drugs and alternative lifestyles. But her touchstone during these confusing years was her great-aunt, who hailed from Texas and had gently guided Jane through many difficult times. Her great-aunt would listen without judging or criticizing when Jane would recount her latest misadventures. The most she would ever say was, "Sometimes, darlin', I guess you just have to rise above yourself." This acceptance and encouragement was one of the sources of Jane's strength and belief in herself. She finally emerged from those turbulent times and settled into a nice family life and successful career. Every once in a while she still hears her great-aunt's voice reminding her to "rise above yourself."

Those who bless us with this kind of encouragement can invite us to positive change.

Ken Tucker (Gross, 2004), rock and movie critic, told the story of his first mentor. He complained to the music editor of the *Village Voice* that the paper wasn't covering a crucial part of the rock scene—middle-of-the-road rock acts that were playing at the Academy of Music in New York City. The editor told Tucker, "Okay, you cover that scene. Spend a month there and write a review." When Tucker finished writing his review a month later, he dropped it off at the *Village Voice* desk, then immediately went home and called the editor. "It is horrible" was the message he left. "Please just throw it in the trash. I'm sorry." Soon he got a call back from the editor, who told him sternly that he should never again call an editor and put his own work down. "It's a perfectly good piece and now I am going to work with you to make it better." The editor went on to change every sentence in the review, and did that with Tucker's subsequent reviews. But he believed in Tucker's talent and potential. That was a mentor who blessed.

Allan Gurganus (1997) said in an interview in the magazine *Bomb:*

> Each of us has an inherent capacity for providing other people with bridges or transitions or assistance that can serve an angelic function. People have done that for me. Call them freelance Fairy Godmothers, but we all have been in positions where we were feeling hopeless and despondent, stuck, and somebody came along at exactly the right time, sometimes people we didn't know, and said, "A piano is about to fall on you from the fourth floor" or "Call this person" or "Here's a job" or "Come to bed with me." There are junctures in our lives where people can serve supernal and angelic functions for us. Without half knowing!

Here's an example from the clinical arena:

Client: I criticize myself. It's like there's this negative voice in my head undermining everything I do by telling me how bad it was and what I did wrong. I am losing my confidence at work and there are lots of politics there. If I slip up, others will take advantage of that slip and use it to destroy my agendas.

Therapist: So, there are those negative tapes and voices. Is there anyone that you have found gives you positive support and tapes?

Cl: When I was growing up, I read a biography of Eleanor Roosevelt. People attacked and criticized her all the time and she became stronger because of it. She said something like, "No one can make you feel bad without your permission." I've always liked that. I guess I have an Eleanor Roosevelt tape that has helped me get this far.

Th: What do you think you could do to turn down the volume on the negative tape and turn up the Eleanor Roosevelt tape?

Cl: I guess I could find that saying of hers and tape it up at work and at home. That would help.

POSITIVE AND NEGATIVE ROLE MODELS FROM AFAR

We may not need to meet our role models to have them help us change. I have several personal and professional role models I have learned quite a bit from but have never met.

I knew I wanted a long career as a teacher and writer and one of the first people I modeled myself on was the rock musician Sting. I read an interview of him early in my career in which he was asked how he had thrived as a musician and avoided the "rock star" trap. He said he had thought about it a lot when he was dreaming of becoming a star. To paraphrase, he said the blueprints for how to destroy your life as a rock musician are already there, he said. Look at Janis Joplin, Elvis Presley, and Jimi Hendrix. Here's how you do it: Go on the road too much and lose touch with everyday real life; eat bad food; take drugs to get to sleep after that exhilarating concert that ends late at night; take drugs to get up the next day; ditch all your old friends that know you as the regular person you are and surround yourself with sycophants who will tell you you are the greatest person in the world with no flaws. "Why would I bother to repeat that scenario?" Sting asked. It's been done. I am trying to forge a new model in which I not only survive, but constantly challenge myself and reinvent myself through a long career. I have watched Sting from afar and, like one of my other models, Paul Simon, he has accomplished his task. His music is continually renewing itself and he has achieved longevity in his career. He seems to have a stable home and family life.

Sean did not like or respect his father when he was growing up. His father never seemed to miss an opportunity to put his kids or his wife down. Sean's father also failed in every business or career venture he undertook, but it was always "they" who were to blame for his father's failures. His father would rant against the "damn Jews" who had all the money, the "damn niggers" who were ruining the country, the "f-ing politicians" who were always stacking the deck and taxes against the little guy. When Sean grew up, he and his wife adopted several special-needs children of different races. Sean took care to give each of his children the message that they were perfect the way they were and that he believed in their value and potential. Every time he found himself being impatient or discouraged, he would remember his father and remind himself to take responsibility for himself and to be patient and kind to others. His father became a reverse role model for him.

As writer Dennis Bagehot has said: "The great pleasure in life is doing what other people say you cannot do." Negative role models and people who make negative predictions can sometimes be the source of many positive changes in our lives.

Here is an illustration of identifying and using mentors in the change process:

> Client: I just procrastinate making that difficult phone call to my boyfriend to tell him it is over. I feel bad because he thinks everything is okay and I know I can't go on like this anymore. I don't really love him and staying with him isn't good for me or for him. But I feel so guilty and avoid the hard conversation.
>
> Therapist: Have you ever known anyone who was good at having the hard conversations?
>
> Cl: Hmm, let me think. I'm not sure I know . . . oh, yeah, I had a girlfriend in high school who was very straightforward. She just said what was on her mind and let the chips fall where they may. We talked about it once and she said two things that

struck me, because they were so true but so different from how I was thinking about it. She said, eventually, the truth was going to come out, so why not get to it earlier rather than later. The other thing she said was that when you avoid saying the tough thing, you often double other people's hurt. They might be hurt because you don't like them but doubly hurt that you didn't think enough of them to tell them. I guess I just have to make that call. I think she's right. If it were me, I would want my boyfriend to tell me as soon as he knew rather than prolonging it. I guess I owe him that much.

QUESTIONS TO ASK IN RESPECT TO MENTORING AND BLESSINGS

Who has inspired you?

Who has believed or believes the best of you?

Who has encouraged you?

Who are your role models, people who you would like to emulate?

Who are your negative role models, people who you are sure you do not want to be like?

Have you ever had mentors, people who helped you navigate some area of life or work? What did you learn from them? How did you change from those relationships?

Do you know anyone or know of anyone who would handle this situation better than you are handling it? What would they do or how would they view it?

MENTOR/MODEL METHOD OF CHANGE:
A SUMMARY

- Identify people who have been negative role models for you, people who illustrated a way of living or handling things that you did not want to emulate.

- Identify people who have cursed you and told you that change was not possible—people who you rebelled against and worked hard to disprove.

- Identify people who believed in or encouraged you in life or during difficult times. Find positive role models who model how to handle difficulties well.

- Determine if you have read about or observed anyone from a distance that could serve as a helpful or negative model for how to change or handle whatever problem you are facing.

CHAPTER SIX

Custom Reframing:

The New Perspective Method of Change

It is not the strongest of the species that survive, nor the most intelligent, but the ones most responsive to change.
—CHARLES DARWIN

Some years ago, I read an article, the source of which is lost to memory. The gist of the authors' approach was to simply shift the perceived meaning of a child's troubling behavior for the parents in an attempt to resolve the problem. If the parents thought the child was depressed, the therapists would suggest that perhaps the child was really angry or was trying to control them. If the child were throwing tantrums, perhaps underneath it all he or she was really sad and had not ever talked about what he or she was sad about. Instead of misbehaving, they might suggest, perhaps their child was emotionally disturbed. The authors reported good success with this method, which they called "Bad or Sad or Mad." It didn't seem to matter which new frame of reference they chose, as long as the frame was a new one that led to different responses. These different responses and actions from the parents seemed to be the thing that correlated with positive change.

This, in essence, is an illustration of the "new perspective" method of change: Help people change their point of view or focus of attention. In therapy jargon, this is often called *reframing*: putting a new frame of reference around the same set of facts. This chapter shows several ways to make changes in viewpoints and perspective to make change happen.

In Santa Fe, where I live, there is a ubiquitous bumper sticker that reads: DON'T BELIEVE EVERYTHING YOU THINK. I admire a quotation by Emile Chartier: "Nothing is as dangerous as an idea when it is the only one you have." This chapter contends that change can happen when people challenge the way they are currently thinking or framing situations or when they shift their focus of attention.

I told the story in an earlier chapter of how I walked myself step by step out of being shy. Actions created that change, but the impetus to take those actions occurred when I came across a new notion about shyness that I read somewhere. Perhaps I wasn't shy as a fixed or set quality; maybe merely learned to "do" shy. That idea was enough to open me to the possibility that shyness was something I could change, which indeed I have over these many years since I first came across the notion.

CHALLENGE IMPOSSIBILITY VIEWS

In terms of creating change, any shift in thinking or attention when you are stuck—what I have called changing the viewing—can be helpful. But there are some common views that seem to impede change. These are views that suggest that change is impossible.

Martin Seligman (1998) indicated one of the frames of reference of people who are less likely to be depressed than others. They have the sense that their situations are changeable rather than set. This is one way to create change through changing points of view. Search for the aspect of whatever situation you want to change that is changeable or start with the assumption that the situation is changeable.

I have encountered variations of this view that change is impossible in couples, in families, and among therapists. In couples, one partner decides that the other is unchangeable or that the marriage itself will never change. Usually this view leads to wanting to break up, since it is so discouraging. It's the same in families. I once had an adoptive family tell me that their child was too damaged and uncontrollable and they wanted to give him back. I managed to calm them down and we went on to create change with this supposedly unchangeable child (in part by changing the parents' response to his misbehavior). Among therapists, this often takes the form that the client is resistant or too damaged by his or her genetics or traumas to be able to change. I have heard psychiatrists tell patients that they will have to be on medication the rest of their lives. I have had to bite my tongue when I hear these pronouncements because I want to say that only God knows the future and I fear the psychiatrists are getting themselves mixed up with God. Bertrand Russell said: "In all affairs it's a healthy thing now and then to hang a question mark on the things you have long taken for granted."

There could be a simple fix for these "delusions of certainty" and a way to put the question mark back in. It would be the simple insertion of some variation on the word *may* or *might,* what I call a possibility word. If the psychiatrists had said to the patient, "You might need to be on this medication the rest of your life," it would at least open the possibility that the patient might not need to be on the medication at some point, that change could happen. If the parents of the adoptive child had said, "We are concerned that our son might never change or stop misbehaving or that he may be too damaged to get better," it would go a long way to not only creating hope but spurring a search for solutions.

I usually validate the possibility that change might not occur or that it might be impossible when I encounter someone who holds this view. Then I add the other possibility, that change might occur or be possible: "Your wife may never change and this marriage may not be salvageable, but let's try some things to find out whether that's really true or not." "Your patient may need to be on mediation for the rest of his life, but there may be new developments in treatment or our understanding of the nature of the problem that may lead to other directions of intervention or solution." Since the impossibility view is included and validated, the person does not have to defend or fight with me about that. Then I gently introduce possibility into the situation.

CHANGE YOUR FOCUS OF ATTENTION

When I was a child and would cross my eyes, my mother would utter the classic parent line, "Don't do that, your eyes might get stuck that way." In a similar way, I would say to people, "Be careful where you fix your attention. You views might get stuck that way." William James held: "[O]ur experience is what we attend to." When you want to create change, try shifting attention. Wherever or how you've been focusing attention, try shifting it in another direction.

There are many places our attention becomes focused without our even noticing it. I often focus on the future. I never noticed it until my wife pointed it out to me after several years together. Below is a short list of things you could try in order to shift your attention, with some examples to illustrate how they might be put into practice.

Change Your Orientation in Time

Past to Present

A client of mine was continually remembering her nice childhood and lamenting the fact that life was not as it used to be. In therapy, we began a series of exercises designed to get her to focus more on the present. She started a gratitude journal that involved listing five things that had happened that day for which she was grateful. She also began to practice mindfulness, noticing how often her thoughts went to the past and how much she complained. She also began slowing down her eating, stopping to taste her food, as she had a tendency to overeat and to eat unconsciously. The net effect of these things was a rise in her general level of peace and happiness.

Past to Future

A traumatized client learned to imagine a better future every time traumatic memories from her past intruded.

Present to Past

A client who was very self-critical began to deliberately focus on things she had done well in the past when she found herself criticizing herself for something she had just done.

Present to Future

A client who was homeless and jobless found herself getting depressed about her situation and then giving up looking for work. She discovered that having a dream of living in a house someday gave her the motivation to get out and look for a job.

Future to Past

A man whose wife complained that he was always living in his dreams and avoiding talking about any issues wrote a memoir of his growing-up years that detailed many of the issues in his past and how they had led to some of his current problems. His wife was relieved to see that he could acknowledge problems and deal with the past. He also found it helpful to make some connections to the past and it helped him begin to shift some persistent and long-term problem patterns.

Future to Present

A couple who had gotten themselves into serious debt by always thinking that their financial ship would come in and save them someday (they would win the lottery; a relative would die and leave them money; one of them would invent something or write a book that would make them rich; one of their investments would pay off big time) learned to change their focus to the present. The question became: Could they afford this thing right now? If the answer was no, they would save until they could afford it. Only after they had the money in hand would they buy.

There are variations on these shifts. For example, one could change orientations in time and attitude, such as from negative past to positive past, from negative present to positive present, or from negative future to positive future. I had a client who worried a lot and she would tend to imagine the very worst happening in the future as well as miss the good things that had happened or were happening. So we made a rule in therapy: For every worried or negative thing she told me, she had to find one positive thing to say about the present, the past, or the future. She gradually incorporated this pattern into her thinking, which became more balanced between positives and negatives. She gradually became much less anxious.

CHANGE INTERNAL TO EXTERNAL ORIENTATION AND VICE VERSA

I heard a story once that a psychiatrist had a patient in his office who was actively hallucinating, talking about ghosts and demons and cosmic rays coming through the walls. The psychiatrist asked the patient to stop for a moment and just feel the wood grain on the desk. The hallucinations and delusional talk ceased. Why? Because the patient had been caught up in his inner world and the psychiatrist had reoriented the patient's attention to the external world and reality.

I have done similar things. A client of mine used to get lost in her abuse memories and flashbacks so intensely that she would forget that she was in my office and would not even be able to hear me when I spoke to her. After several incidents of this and her being lost alone in torturous memories, we worked out a simple procedure. When she would begin to slide into the memories, she would reach out with her little finger and I would grab on to it. This had the effect of keeping her connected to the current external reality and she would no longer collapse completely into the past and her inner world so we could continue our therapeutic work.

Of course, there are times when clients are too externally oriented and they lose touch with themselves. I had a client who was prone to dissociation after a childhood and early adult years of abuse and a date rape. She was getting better through therapy, but she had discovered that as soon as a man expressed sexual interest in her, she would lose herself in the experience. She had had unprotected sex several times during the course of treatment and would later become fearful and upset with herself for letting this happen. Finally she made a plan. She set an alarm in the other room when the man she was dating came home with her. It was timed to go off 10 minutes after they had begun petting, which was usually a little while before they had intercourse. She got up to turn off the alarm and that gave her time to think. When she returned to the bedroom, she brought a condom with her and had her partner put it on.

CHANGE INTERNAL TO EXTERNAL CAUSATION AND VICE VERSA

All too often, women who are physically or sexually abused somehow think it is their fault. Their partners might tell them this or they might just be prone to self-blame. Part of the treatment for this and other forms of abuse is to help victims realize that they are not to blame.

It is often the opposite for those who are perpetrating the abuse. "She made me do it. She wouldn't stop nagging." I heard a rapist say, "She really wanted it, but women are programmed by society not to admit they want it." For these people, what can open up change is to shift the cause from external to internal. I had a man who said, after he had hit his wife, "I hit her. It was a reaction." There was a subtle shift of responsibility and cause to the external in that statement. I responded simply, "You hit her. Even if there was a provocative situation, it is still you who chose to strike out." He sat in silence for a moment and then said, "Yes."

CHANGE VIEW OF THE PERMANENCE OF PROBLEMS

Another of the factors and attitudes that Seligman (1998) found in people who tended to be less depressed was that they believed the problems they were facing were not permanent. They would use phrases like, "This is a difficult phase I am going through" or "I can't wait until this depression passes." People who were more depressed tended to see the problem as permanent: "I have depression" or "I am messed up."

Therapists can help clients move from a sense of permanence to a more temporary view of the problem in several ways, using language. One is to assume that there will be a time when the problem is resolved and speak congruently with that view. "After you come out of this depression, how do you think your relationship with your friend will change?" one might ask. Or "When you get through this difficult period, how do you think it will have changed you?"

Another linguistic maneuver is to avoid using terms that imply that the problem is a permanent quality or part of the person's makeup. I sometimes say something like, "You have been living in depression-land for some time. Do you remember what it was like to live outside of that place?" Or borrowing a tool from an approach called narrative therapy: "When depression moved in with you, how much of your life did it take over? How could you get some of your life back from depression?"

ACCEPT RATHER THAN TRY TO CHANGE SOMETHING

Sometimes, paradoxical as it may seem, accepting things is the best approach to change. If you have done all you can do to make change or you find that struggling to change something creates more problems, the best path might be surrender and acceptance. Carl Rogers held: "The curious paradox is that when I accept myself just as I am, then I can change." Sometimes the acceptance leads to a breakthrough in being able to change. At other times, just accepting creates a sense of peace, which dissolves the problematic sense of things.

John Gottman (1995) found in his research on happy couples in long-term relationships that the couples eventually came to the conclusion that there were some issues they were not going to resolve and came to a sense of acceptance and peace in those areas.

A client of mine came into a session very excited. He had just read an article and determined that he had adult attention deficit disorder. For years he had thought he was lazy or stupid, but now realized that he wasn't such a bad or irresponsible person. As he came to accept this over the next few months, he found ways to work with himself instead of berating himself. He became much more peaceful. He didn't want to take medications or even work on improving his attentional abilities. Acceptance brought peace.

EXPRESS GRATITUDE/RECOGNIZE WHAT YOU HAVE OR WHAT HAS GONE WELL

Human beings seem biased toward noticing problems and when things are not going well. Perhaps it is a survival thing. If we didn't notice that tiger creeping up on us or hadn't smelled the smoke from a fire, we might have died during our evolution. To counteract that natural orientation, we can begin to deliberately notice what is going well or has gone well. Many religions have a procedure for noticing and expressing what we are grateful for. Shifting from a problem frame to a gratitude frame can create change in our experience or may lead to the conditions for change in that we have more peace of mind and energy with which to approach problems and problem-solving.

A client of mine was unhappy with her life and I told her a story about people I knew who stopped focusing on themselves and began volunteering at an organization that helped others. She decided to try the same route and ended up working for an organization that bought small animals for impoverished people in foreign countries. As she learned more about how much of humanity lived without enough food and shelter, she became more and more grateful for the simple things she had previously taken for granted in her life: accessible high-quality medical care, enough to eat, a warm and soft place to sleep, and so on. She told me that if I recommended this course of action to others of my clients, I would put myself out of business. No one would want therapy. I told her that would be fine with me.

GET A BIGGER OR SMALLER PERSPECTIVE

Sometimes change can come from shifting our perspectives on our lives and the problems we face. I have had clients imagine that they are thinking about their current situation at the age of 90. How would they view it then? Often the problem seems much less troubling or not as significant from that distance. Search for a larger perspective and find out whether that creates change or not.

A client was frustrated with his wife who, in his view, was too involved with her mother's problems. His mother-in-law had been verbally abusive to his wife in her childhood and the pattern continued into the present. He couldn't understand why his wife would spend hours on the phone listening her mother's complaints, given their history. His wife would tell him that he didn't understand

and that family was family. He and his wife would have terrible arguments over this issue. The man was religious and I asked him to imagine that he was having a conversation with Jesus about the problem. What would Jesus say? He instantly smiled and said, "Jesus would love her no matter what she did. He accepted everyone just as they were." He went home that evening and apologized to his wife for criticizing her and not understanding her relationship with her mother. Over time, as he held his tongue, his wife set better boundaries with her mother on her own. Getting a bigger perspective, derived from his religious faith, helped this man make a positive change.

On the other hand, sometimes we get overwhelmed by the size of our problems. A couple I worked with was dealing with the aftermath of one of the partners having been indicted for stealing money from the company for which she worked. She was involved in a court case and the couple had to come up with money for a lawyer and to make reparations to the company. They were feeling overwhelmed by all that they had to do and deal with as individuals and as a couple. I told them the story behind the title of a book by Anne Lamott (1995) called *Bird by Bird.* Lamott's younger brother was panicked at the end of a vacation and confessed tearfully to his father that he had procrastinated doing a long book report on North American birds. Now he had only one day and there was no way he would finish the report. His father insisted he work on it. "How will I get it done?" cried Lamott's brother. "Bird by bird, son, bird by bird," replied the father. After that, whenever this couple in therapy felt overwhelmed, they would turn to each other and say, "Bird by bird." That helped.

Below is a handout I give to clients to help them make changes in their perspectives or thinking:

DON'T BELIEVE EVERYTHING YOU THINK: HOW TO CHALLENGE AND ESCAPE THE DOMINATION OF UNHELPFUL THOUGHTS

You Are Not Your Mind

You are bigger than your mind, but sometimes it seems as though your mind has you or thoughts are thinking you.

Disindentification—Recognize that your mind is just your mind and your thoughts are just your thoughts; they are not equal to your identity.

Externalizing—Treat your thoughts as if they were an external person.

Mindfulness—Just notice thoughts or patterns of thinking rather than believing them.

Challenge Thoughts

Use counterarguments—Challenge unhelpful thoughts with facts that contradict them.

Make slight shifts in your self-talk or thoughts—Instead of all-or-nothing self-talk, change it to mostly, usually, rarely, and so on; instead of "why," change it to "how can I" and so on.

Just the Facts

Use observational/sensory-based descriptions—This helps to separate interpretations and imposed meanings from what happens; only describe what you could see or hear on a videotape about the situation or yourself.

Go with the Thoughts Rather Than Fight or Oppose Them

Accept and soften toward one's thoughts—Don't oppose or react; opposing gives the unhelpful thoughts energy. What you resist tends to persist.

Exaggerate—Amplify negative or fearful thoughts until they are absurd or lose their power.

Get into Dialogue and out of Monologue

With another/others—Talking to another person or several others can sometimes get you on a new track, provide a reality check, and help you get perspective on your thoughts.

With self/thoughts—Instead of accepting, fighting with, or being dominated by unhelpful thoughts, engage in a dialogue with yourself or the thoughts and, as in conversations with others, new thoughts or perspectives might occur.

Take Action

Do something that is incompatible with the unhelpful thought—Take an action that wouldn't be expected given the unhelpful thought.

Do something to refute the unhelpful thought— Engage in some action that would disprove the unhelpful thought.

*Action can help you get unstuck and move out of the thought—*Don't just sit there, do something. Being in a different environment, moving your physical body, and other actions can sometimes break you out of your mental rut.

In human life, many things are beyond our control. But we have some freedom. We can choose how we eat and we can choose what to focus our attention on and how we make sense of the world. By exercising those freedoms, we can create change in our lives.

QUESTIONS TO ASK TO HELP CLIENTS GET A NEW PERSPECTIVE

Where have you developed the idea that you, another person, or your problem situation cannot change? How can you challenge that?

What are you typically paying attention to or noticing in the problem situation?

What does this typical focus of attentiion distract you from, or what else could you pay attention to?

Where do you usually focus your thinking in the problem situation: the past, the present, the future? How can you shift to any other time orientation?

Do you have a sense that you have an internal locus of control (that is, that you influence or cause

things to happen), or do you think your life is
determined by others, or the world? How could
you challenge or shift your current orientation in
this regard?

Where might it be helpful for you to accept rather than
try to change something in the problem situation?

Where could attaining a sense of gratitude or appre-
ciation help you in your problem situation?

How could you either see the bigger picture, get a
broader perspective, or narrow your focus to
something smaller in the problem situation?

NEW PERSPECTIVE METHOD OF CHANGE: A SUMMARY

Change the perspective by:

• challenging the idea that change is impossible

• changing where you focus your attention in the
problem situation

• changing your orientation in time

  ◦ change focus from the past to the present

  ◦ change focus from the past to the future

  ◦ change focus from the present to the past

  ◦ change focus from the present to the future

  ◦ change focus from the future to the past

  ◦ change focus from the future to the present

• changing your explanation about what causes your
problem from internal cause to external cause or
vice versa

- accepting rather than fighting against or trying to change something
- developing or recalling a sense of gratitude about your situation or appreciating what has gone well
- seeing the bigger picture or narrowing your focus to a smaller piece of their problem situation

CHAPTER SEVEN

Residential Psychoanalysis:

The Relationship Path to Change

A pessimist is a man who has been compelled to live with an optimist.
—Elbert Hubbard

This chapter shows how some relationships can be powerful pathways to change. Like coming in contact with a new culture and learning not only new perspectives and possibilities, but also becoming aware of one's own biases and unexamined beliefs, truths and patterns, relationships can be a powerful change environment.

RELATIONSHIPS AS VEHICLES FOR CHANGE

When I was on a book tour publicizing one of my earlier books, I was met at the airport by a guide who chauffeured me around town to various interviews. In the course of our travels, he told me his story. He had dropped out of high school when he was informed as a sophomore that he was currently number 277 out of 278 students and that he would probably not graduate. He headed to the big city at the age of 15 and got a job as a gofer at a big-city newspaper. The older reporters took a liking to him and got him a fake ID so he could go drinking with them and they mentored him in the art of being a newspaper reporter. He drank hard and lived hard for the next 15 years. His preferred drink was brandy and he was usually drunk every night of the week. He had several relationships with women and continued his late-night drinking and partying life through them. At the age of 30, he met the woman of his dreams and they began to date. After several months, though, she gave him an ultimatum: Stop drinking or they were through. He never had a moment's hesitation, he told me. He stopped drinking from that moment on. He was still married to his true love and had been sober since the day she made the ultimatum. He wryly observed that AA might work for some people, but for him it was his wife.

Now we all know how hard it is to stop drinking, but this fellow showed that sometimes relationships, if they are important enough to us, trump even serious addictions and dependencies.

Erickson told the story of the small town in Wisconsin where he grew up. A former resident of the town was released from prison and soon petty crimes began to happen all over town. People's businesses were broken into and cash was stolen. Houses were burgled. Everyone suspected Joe, the ex-con, but nothing could be proved.

One day a wagon carrying one of the town's prettiest girls was stopped by Joe when he stepped out in front of the horses pulling the wagon. The young girl asked to be let by. Joe said, "Only if you will agree to go to the dance with me." The girl replied simply, "If you are a gentleman." From that day on, the local crime wave ceased. Joe went on to marry that girl and they had a family and lived in peace in that community for many years. Erickson's comment on the situation was, "If people can suddenly develop problems [such as phobias], they can just as suddenly change" (O'Hanlon & Hexum, 1991).

I was once working with an adolescent who was getting bad grades, using drugs, and being defiant at home. I wasn't making much progress, so after several sessions I asked him to bring in his two or three closest friends to the next session. He agreed. When I explained what I was up to, trying to find out about the situation and find some way to help him change, he denied there were any issues, although the school and his parents had provided me with ample evidence of problems. His friends began to talk to him, telling him that indeed he was in trouble and that they had all been worried about him and his future. They detailed numerous incidents in which he had been high and could have been seriously hurt. Confronted with not only this evidence, but with their concern, he agreed to work with me to make some changes in these areas.

It has become fashionable in therapy circles to hold two beliefs: (a) You can't change another person, only yourself; and (b) you shouldn't change yourself for a relationship or for another person. I don't buy either of those ideas. We change each other all the time. People change for those they love quite often.

Now there is a crucial distinction that should be made here. The best conditions for change come with acceptance. "We cannot change anything unless we accept it," claimed Carl Jung. The same holds true in relationships. The relationships that call forth positive change are those that provide a ground of accepting the person. I tell my clients: You are okay, but some of your behaviors and points of view suck and don't work. If a person feels accepted and not blamed and critiqued at the core level of who they are, they are much more likely to be open to change at a more superficial level.

Harville Hendrix and Helen LaKelly Hunt (2004), originators of Imago Therapy, held that everything you need is available through a long-term committed relationship. Their basic premise is that, over time, one's partner both holds and brings to the foreground unfinished issues and neglected and devalued aspects of people. Hendrix and Hunt encourage people never to get divorces or to break up with their long-term partners because eventually whatever issues led to the trouble in one's current relationship will surface in future relationships. One might as well stay and work them out in the current one.

I agree that the issues can indeed be worked out in a relationship, but one must find the right relationship in which to do this work. It must be with a person who is trustworthy and well intentioned and who is willing to engage in such a process. Some people are not up for this work in a relationship. It wouldn't work in relationships where there is not enough basic love or commitment. But I take Hendrix and Hunt's point that many of us, especially in these days of instant everything, are all too likely to run away from the difficult process of working things through. I have joked that being in a relationship with a strong and loving partner or friend can be like being in residential psychoanalysis 24 hours a day, 365 days of the year: It can both push you up against everything you don't want to know about yourself and that is unconscious for you, and it can help you resolve many unfinished issues from childhood.

Usually at the beginning of a romantic relationship, we idealize our partner. Over time, some of the very things we fell in love with begin to irritate us or drive us crazy. If we stay engaged, though, as Hendrix and Hunt suggest, we can move through this phase to another: that of deep acceptance of the other person.

A couple consulted me for marital problems. They had emigrated from another country and, for legal and financial reasons, they had to stay married. They worked together in a business they owned together that was housed in the lower floor of their home. They spent most of their time bickering, sniping at each other, and generally feeling miserable. They were continually suspicious of the other's motives, attributing the worst intentions even to the other's most innocent comments and actions. I worked with them for a time and was able to get them to bicker much less and to be less suspicious of each other. But they were never able to feel love or affection for each other. They were satisfied with the therapy when we ended but it had bothered me that we couldn't seem to resuscitate the love and friendship they had had earlier in their marriage. About a year later, they phoned me and told me that they were now deeply in love again and thanked me for the work I had done to keep them together. They had stumbled on the Imago Therapy idea that any time your partner upsets you, it is a potential gift—you only need to recognize and use that gift. It can be a gift because it alerts you to some unfinished business or some unhealed wound. They became fascinated with this idea and had decided that since they were each so good at upsetting the other, they had married the exact person who could facilitate their personal growth. From Imago and some other reading they had done, they found ways to soften toward each other when the other was upset. Using these procedures, they developed a level of compassion and support for each other that grew into a new and deep love.

RELATIONSHIPS AS VEHICLES FOR ILLUMINATING ASSUMPTIONS AND PATTERNS

> *A man may be a fool and not know it, but not if he is married.*
> —H. L. Mencken

Relationships can illuminate flaws in one's approach to life by exposing one to other ways of thinking and doing things. Your partner also gets to observe your patterns over the long term and to see both the positive and negative consequences of those patterns. My wife, Steffanie, has lovingly pointed out to me a pattern of impulsiveness and my inability to anticipate potentially negative consequences. This is not always a problem, but when it is, it gets me in hot water and takes a lot of time, energy, or money to clean up. I have learned that it is worth the effort to slow down and discuss my enthusiasms of the moment with her to get her perspective on things. As a consequence, I have decided not to go ahead with some projects and to alter others. I have also begun to incorporate an "inner Steffanie" in my psyche, who occasionally asks the kinds of good questions Steffanie does and gives me a better perspective on things. I think I have served the same function for her in helping her to recognize and shift a few of her patterns and biases as well.

Steffanie has told me that she has learned something from me in terms of jumping into a project rather than waiting for all the conditions to be perfect or waiting not to be afraid. This has helped her in her career as an artist.

I grew up in a messy house, not dirty, just messy. Papers abounded and things always seemed to be in disarray. Not surprisingly, my house when I was an adult looked much like my parents' house. Steffanie preferred a tidy house. We finally reached a compromise. I could keep my office as messy as I wanted but the rest of the house would stay tidy. I found I liked a tidy house and my office is well on the way to being tidy as I write this. I can actually find things in it.

So we can learn and model on things that are not natural for us through relationships. We can also learn to recognize and change deeply unconscious patterns.

John was raised in a family that used a lot of teasing. When he and June first got together, she enjoyed his humor, but after a time she realized he used that teasing humor to indirectly communicate that he was unhappy about something in their relationship or to subtly shift the blame to her for something about which he felt guilty. When June first pointed this out to John, he used his humor to deflect it: Thank you, Sigmund Freud. But June persisted. This was not helping their relationship. It didn't lead to solving problems. It just created hurt and left things unresolved. Over time, especially after some visits with his family of origin, John began to see the cruelty in his family that came out through teasing. He agreed to work on changing the pattern. At times, he would get defensive right after June would point out that he was using teasing in this unhealthy way, but he learned that she was usually right. Gradually he learned to check the impulse to say something teasing or cutting and think about what he really wanted to say that might be masked by the teasing.

June used gentle confrontation but was careful to reassure John that she loved him and believed he was better than his behavior. This combination of acceptance and challenge is usually the most successful approach.

Over time, couples often come to resemble each other emotionally and psychologically, probably through this process of incorporating things from their partners and modeling on their partners. A Creole proverb suggests: "Tell me who you love and I'll tell you who you are."

FINDING OR CREATING A "THERAPEUTIC RELATIONSHIP" THAT CAN HELP YOU GROW

To some extent, finding such a relationship can be a matter of luck or fate. Some people find one and some people don't (and really, some people don't want this kind of relationship).

Some years ago, I cowrote a book called *Love Is a Verb*" (O'Hanlon & Hudson, 1994) in which the main premise was that love can be created, maintained, and grown through actions. I have come to modify that view a little. I use the analogy of a garden. It does take actions to maintain and grow a garden—the right amount of water, weeding, cultivation of the soil. But there is some part of the plant-growing process that is beyond our control—it is a matter of nature and chemistry. I have a similar view of relationships. Love is a verb, except when it is a noun. There is some part of these growth-enhancing relationships that is chemistry and a mystery—that is the noun part. Find someone you are willing to hang around with the rest of your life, someone you like and respect enough to last after the lust and infatuation have faded a bit. When you find such a relationship, then it is a matter of the verb part, that is, there are things you can do to foster this kind of growth-inducing relationship.

- Accept that person as they are, not trying to change them at core. That means not diagnosing or labeling your partner, and when you ask for change, focusing mostly on their actions rather than their qualities or feelings.
- Be rigorous and ruthlesslessly compassionate when your partner messes up or isn't living with integrity or from their highest aspects. Call them on their mess-ups or lack of integrity, never blaming, but reminding them of their best self and potential.
- Be patient with yourself and your partner to allow time for change and for understanding to occur.
- Be rigorous as well in examining whether you have a part in your partner's problems or mess-ups. If not, don't worry about it, but if so, fess up and clean up your part.
- Stay in the conversation and the relationship, even when you feel like giving up, giving in, or leaving.

QUESTIONS TO ASK TO ILLUMINATE CHANGE THROUGH INTIMATE RELATIONSHIPS

In what way does your partner appear like an alien to you? What can you learn or model from that difference?

How does your partner drive you crazy or push your buttons regularly? What could that illuminate about unfinished or unresolved aspects of your life?

How have you changed in positive ways through
   relationships?

What habits or traits does your partner or friend
    have that you would like to develop more in your
    own life?

Who matters enough to you to influence to change?

How might your partner represent or carry one of
    your "missing pieces?"

THE RELATIONSHIP PATH TO CHANGE:
A SUMMARY

- Relationships can be powerful vehicles for change,
  providing motivation and intimate challenges.

- The myths in therapy and in our society are that
  you can never change anyone else, only yourself,
  and that you shouldn't change for anyone else.

- Find someone who influences you, who matters,
  and use them as leverage for bringing about
  change.

- Paradoxically, sometimes the best way to change
  someone is to accept them as they are.

- Intimate relationships can illuminate unquestioned
  assumptions and ingrained habits and patterns.

- Love is maintained by actions, but is has a strong
  basis in chemistry and compatibility.

CHAPTER EIGHT

Becoming Yourself:

How to Change by Becoming More of Your True Self

I love those who change in order to stay themselves. —BERTOLT BRECHT

It may seem paradoxical, but some people change by reclaiming or rediscovering their true selves. There is some debate as to whether we really have true selves, but most people feel some sense of unease when they feel they are not being true to who they "really are."

It seems to me, as I move solidly into my middle years, that my whole life has been a quest to be who I am. I spent much of the early years either trying to prove myself to the world and myself and or to please others. In these years, I find myself gathering aspects of myself that I have neglected or left behind and easing into a sense of peace and acceptance.

I no longer dream that I will be organized. I suspect that I will always be a bit hyper. I am less and less bothered that I seem to have a large streak of laziness at the core of my life. I have learned to modulate my selfishness so that it isn't too untoward or it doesn't hurt those I love so much.

The most profound journey, I am suggesting, is to live more and more into your own life, into your own skin. Many years ago, I was getting some bodywork done. The practitioner was a friendly acquaintance of mine. He remarked while he was working on me, "Bill, you are not living out to the edges of your earth suit." Despite the New Age jargon, I knew what he meant. I had been systematically socialized in my early years not to live in my body. In my religious upbringing, I was taught that the body was the devil's territory, home of lust and mortal desires. I became intellectual, leading with my head, but often tuning out or not taking care of my body. More than that, I had abandoned other aspects of myself in addition to my body. I was not living out to the edges of my life, my skin, my feelings, my yearnings and particular sensibilities.

I began a quest to reclaim my life and live fully and with integrity. Sometimes when people are having problems, those problems are like stalkers from people's lives who will not give up no matter what change techniques are used. They will not give up until those people reclaim their missing and neglected aspects and begin to live the life they were meant to live.

Kevin was a successful surgeon. He had it all. Good marriage, nice bright good kids. Money. Status. In his forties, Kevin began to mess up his life. He became addicted to pain pills, got caught, and had his medical license put on probation. While in rehab, he began to realize something. He never really wanted to be a doctor. That was his father's dream for him. He quickly suppressed this realization. For a time, things seemed to be going well again—until Kevin began to have panic attacks before he went into surgery. He was reluctant to take antianxiety medications due to his past addictions, so he sought psychotherapy. When he arrived in my office, instead of the usual questions, my intuition told me to ask, "Do you think you are really supposed to be a doctor or was there something else you were supposed to do with your life?" Kevin seemed stunned, but he said that I had just asked him the most important question of his life. What the truth was, and he found this hard to say because it would turn his life upside down, was that he had always wanted to be a singer. He had the talent, but had decided early on that this was an unrealistic dream; he had chosen the more lucrative and stable life of a doctor instead. Over the course of the next few months, Kevin spoke with his wife and kids about the change he wanted to make. To his surprise, they were very supportive. His father thought he was crazy, but his mother secretly called him and expressed her support. He had to stop speaking to his father for some time because his father was undermining his confidence and belittling his dream. He went into a studio and made a CD and set up a Web site to sell the CD. He began performing in local clubs. The panic attacks stopped. He gradually worked himself out of his surgical practice, putting aside money to support his family while he changed careers. He was happier than he had ever been and his wife and kids reported that he was much more loving and available. He told me that I had saved him thousands of dollars in midlife crisis costs by asking him that one crucial question.

I will end with a quotation from Anaïs Nin: "One discovers that destiny can be directed, that one does not have to remain in bondage to the first imprint made on childhood sensibilities. Once the deforming mirror has been smashed, there is a possibility of wholeness. There is a possibility of joy."

QUESTIONS TO ASK TO DETERMINE WHETHER OR NOT YOU ARE BEING YOUR TRUE SELF:

Do you feel comfortable with yourself, in your skin and in your life?

Do you have a sense that you are doing the right work?

Do you have a sense that you have left some significant pieces of yourself behind or have lost them?

Do you fantasize about running away and starting a new life with a new identity?

If you died tomorrow, would you be satisfied with how your life went?

If money or obligations were not issues, what would you be doing in your life?

CHANGE BY BECOMING MORE OF YOUR TRUE SELF: A SUMMARY

Sometimes we change by returning to or rediscovering who we really are. This may involve reclaiming lost pieces, aspects, or dreams we have misplaced along the way in order to stay safe, be loved, fit in, or try to control our lives.

CHAPTER NINE

How Not to Change:

Eleven Strategies for Staying Stuck, with a Special Bonus Section on How to Invite Others Not to Change

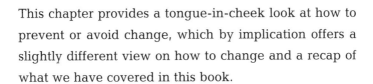

There is no sin punished more implacably by nature than the sin of resistance to change. —ANNE MORROW LINDBERGH

This chapter provides a tongue-in-cheek look at how to prevent or avoid change, which by implication offers a slightly different view on how to change and a recap of what we have covered in this book.

1. DON'T LISTEN TO ANYBODY

We sometimes get stuck in our own little ways of thinking about or doing things. Other people can be helpful in giving us a new perspective or new possibilities. They say that travel broadens the mind. I think it broadens by exposing us to cultures, thoughts, and habits much different from our usual ones. Travel in foreign climes can also challenge the assumptions we have and never even notice. Listening to others can do the same. Read books, listen to tapes, talk to friends, talk to people you would never think you would talk to. Expose yourself to new thoughts.

2. LISTEN TO EVERYBODY

At the same time, letting other people's views of the world or what is right for you dominate your life can put you in danger of losing yourself and your sensibilities. Listen to others but continue to check in with yourself to find out what has integrity and rings true to you. It can be easy to go along with the crowd and follow received, commonly held views and trends. Be careful of swallowing influential people's ideas whole. Digest them yourself. Mentors and leaders can be wise and they can also be wrong (or self-serving).

3. ENDLESSLY ANALYZE AND DON'T MAKE ANY CHANGES

It's fine to understand what is going on with you, others, and the world, but be careful of the analysis paralysis trap. I knew early on in my writing life that I was prone to procrastinating. If I had followed my natural tendencies, I would have read a lot about writing, gone to writing workshops, and thought about what I was going to write for years before putting pen to paper (or fingers to keyboard). I decided to just jump in feet first and begin writing. So far, so good (this is my 24th book). I did eventually read those writing books and go to writing workshops to improve my craft. I discovered that some of my writing habits break all the rules. I discovered what worked for me: to write and not worry about the rules.

Sportswear maker Nike's ad advised: *Just do it.* That will work to create change in most situations (of course, except when it doesn't; then you should probably follow the dictum: Don't just do something, stand there). The sailor's maxim "You can't steer a ship until it is moving" tells us that you must be doing something to create change. You can always make course corrections once you begin if you see you are heading in the wrong direction. "An ounce of action is worth a ton of theory," said Friedrich Engels.

Woody Allen's character in *Annie Hall* vowed that he was giving his psychotherapy 20 years and if it still hadn't worked, he was planning to visit Lourdes in search of a miracle. I would advise heading for Lourdes a lot sooner. Woody might have some interesting and change-inducing experiences along the way.

Often doing something leads to new insights as conditions change in response to actions you take. Analysis might arise by making change instead of the other way around.

4. BLAME OTHERS FOR YOUR ACTIONS OR PROBLEMS

Not everything is everybody else's fault. If you find that that is your usual stance or interpretation, try imagining that you had a part in creating this situation. Seligman (1998) did a lot of research showing that people who had a sense that they influenced the events of their lives were more likely to be happy and less likely to be depressed. So even if it is an illusion, imagine that you have some control and choice about what happens in your life.

Barry Beck, New York Ranger hockey player, was asked who started a brawl during the NHL's Stanley Cup play-offs. He replied, "We have only one person to blame, and that's each other" (Pritchett, 1998, p. 47).

5. BLAME YOURSELF OR PUT YOURSELF DOWN REGULARLY

On the other hand, you are not always to blame. Putting yourself down regularly is probably something you took on long ago as a habit that doesn't serve you well. It can demoralize you and undermine your confidence.

I had a client who had this habit and I could not dissuade him from the notion. The best I could do was to convince him that he did not know definitively that everything was his fault or indicated what a terrible person he was. He agreed to correct his knee-jerk judgment with a different thought: I am not sure whether or not I am to blame or this says something terrible about me. Moving to a more neutral stance helped him avoid becoming some discouraged.

6. KEEP DOING THE SAME THING THAT DOESN'T WORK

Do something different if what you are doing is not working. Remember that one definition of insanity is doing the same thing over and over again and expecting different results.

7. KEEP FOCUSING ON THE SAME THINGS WHEN THAT FOCUS DOESN'T HELP

Try shifting your attention in another direction. They say the only difference between a rut and a grave is the dimensions. Get out of your ruts.

8. KEEP THINKING THE SAME THOUGHTS WHEN THOSE THOUGHTS DON'T HELP

There's nothing as dangerous as an idea when it is the only one you have, claimed Emile Chartier. Don't believe everything you think! (We covered this in detail in Chapter 3.)

9. KEEP PUTTING YOURSELF IN THE SAME UNHELPFUL ENVIRONMENT

While there are ways to transcend one's environment, it is often easier to get the heck out of there (unless that is your usual pattern; in that case, try sticking around).

Some years ago I heard an analogy that relates to this notion. Human beings, like many trees, do not thrive in an environment where there is no water. Being in the presence of blame and negativity is like being in a desert. The crucial difference between a human being and a plant, however, is that humans can get up and walk from the desert to the riverside.

10. KEEP RELATING TO THE SAME UNHELPFUL PEOPLE

It is probably wiser to minimize your contact with people who put you down, who gossip, who are acting in a mean-spirited way, or with whom you regularly end up feeling bad after your encounters with them.

11. PUT MORE IMPORTANCE ON BEING RIGHT THAN ON CHANGING

I worked with a couple who were alienated from each other. They had five children and did not want to, or could not afford to, split up. One of the main sources of tension between them was a conflict about sex. She worked the evening shift and would arrive home about 11:30 P.M. He worked the day shift. She decompressed after she came home by watching half an hour or so of mindless television. Every night he would appear at the bedroom door, open it a crack, look out at her watching television, and ask her whether she would be coming to bed soon. This was code for "I'd like to have sex, but I have to get up early, so could you stop watching television and come in here and have sex?" This pressure would annoy her. She knew perfectly well that he wanted to have sex, as did she, but she needed a few more minutes of decompression. He would then appear at the bedroom door every few minutes, open it a crack, see that she was still watching television, and make a *tsk tsk* noise. This would get her back up and, just to spite him, she would stay up for hours watching television, often falling asleep on the couch.

When they sought my help, I was more direct than I usually am. I found out from her that she was really interested in having sex and that if he would only stop the tsking, she would be much more likely to do so. I told him to stop the tsking for one week. He agreed and complied. After not having sex for months, they had sex three times that week. She initiated sex two of those times and said she enjoyed it.

To my dismay, the next week he began the tsking again, with the same dismal results. I asked him why. He told me he thought he had a right to let her know he disapproved of her staying up late. I told him that he was right, but that was not helping his marriage or his sex life. Would he rather be right than be satisfied or happy? He thought about it and said yes. And that was that. While other areas of their relationship improved, their sex life never did again. Although they stayed together, he reverted to the old annoying behavior and their little evening game continued.

At a certain point, one has to decide whether being right is more important than getting positive results. Someday you may end up being dead right.

SPECIAL BONUS SECTION: HOW TO INVITE OTHERS NOT TO CHANGE

Probably the most effective way you can get others not to change is to blame them. Blaming puts people in a defensive frame of mind. You might get compliance for a time if you have enough power to intimidate (or you hold the purse strings or are physically threatening), but long-term change rarely comes through blaming. Blaming usually comes in two varieties: ascribing bad intentions to others or ascribing bad qualities to others. In the first type of blaming, you might tell others that they are trying to cause trouble or be annoying. Or that they are really trying to get attention. Or that they want to control you. These are attributions of bad intentions. The person may or may not have those intentions, but "mind-reading" them in a way that claims that you know the real truth about their motives and that those motives are less than honorable or good is one of the worst ways to approach people for change.

The second kind of blaming involves judging people's characters or qualities as being bad or flawed in some core way. "You are selfish." "You are a controller." These kinds of generalized assessments again create the worst atmosphere for change.

Another unhelpful thing to do when attempting to create change in others is to invalidate their perceptions and trust in their own sense of things. "You're too sensitive," "That's not the way it was," or "You are crazy." You can disagree with people without invalidating them. "That's not the way I remember it." Or "I had a different sense of it than you did." This way of approaching differences still indicates respect and validation while preserving the difference between your sense and theirs.

An excellent way to keep people from changing is to give them unasked-for advice. This is especially true for therapists. It's back to trying to teach a pig to sing. Every once in a while through the years, my mother would call me up and tell me that one of my siblings was having a hard time. "You're a therapist," she would say. "Call them up and see if you can help them resolve this situation." At first I got hooked and would do it, always with disastrous results. After a while, I would call up my troubled sibling and say, "Mom thinks you need help and I should be the one to give it since I am a therapist. But I am really calling to be your brother. I can help you find a therapist if you think you need one." None of them ever took me up on the offer to help find a therapist, but I avoided the disastrous results I knew by then would have occurred had I offered unsolicited help or advice.

Jay Haley (1991) once said that he spent much of his time trying to restrain therapists from being helpful in situations for which they weren't being asked for help. Therapists, because of their training in recognizing and diagnosing pathology and problems, often see things that could be changed in their clients. Because clients are susceptible to suggestion and the authority of the therapist, they might either comply with this imposition of problems or be convinced that they have problems they do not actually have. People's lives have a sometimes delicate ecological balance to them and there may be unintended consequences of such intrusions and impositions by therapists. The "false-memory" controversy of a few years ago in the therapy field showed the consequences of therapists getting too influential in their ideas about problems clients were not actually bringing up on their own. (The "false-memory" controversy refers to a spate of cases a few years ago in which therapists were accused of influencing clients to "remember" that they were sexually or ritually abused. Some of these cases, when investigated, showed that the abuse that was recalled did not happen. Therapists who became advocates and true believers in widespread abuse and repressed memories tended to elicit these false memories most often. Many families suffered rifts, alienation, and lawsuits from such overzealous and righteous therapists. Some therapists lost their licenses when the facts of the cases were investigated.)

There is also a fine line between being too sympathetic and being unsympathetic. If you just give people complete acceptance of their stuckness, their limitations, or their problems, you might inadvertently help keep them stuck. They might feel justified in not changing, since you have agreed that they are victims or powerless. Adding a bit of challenge to your sympathy can go a long way to creating change.

You can get others to change, contrary to popular belief. But you can also be part of what helps people become more resistant to change and entrenched in their current problem.

SOME QUESTIONS TO CONSIDER IN THE AREA OF NOT CHANGING

Where have you resisted change or been inflexible?

Where have you not been thinking for yourself and been too swayed by others' views of the situation?

Where have you pushed someone else to change in an unhelpful or unsuccessful way?

Where have you created a bad atmosphere for encouraging someone else to change?

In what ways have you been blaming or invalidating someone else that you are hoping will change?

In what ways have you been imposing your own ideas of problems on people and trying to convince them that they have those problems?

In what ways have you been supporting the idea that the person you are trying to help change is a victim and powerless?

In what ways have you been overly supportive and not quite challenging enough?

ELEVEN STRATEGIES FOR STAYING STUCK: A SUMMARY

1. Don't listen to anybody.

2. Listen to everybody.

3. Endlessly analyze and don't make any changes.

4. Blame others for your actions or problems.

5. Blame yourself or put yourself down regularly.

6. Keep doing the same thing that doesn't work.

7. Keep focusing on the same things when that focus doesn't help.

8. Keep thinking the same thoughts when those thoughts don't help.

9. Keep putting yourself in the same unhelpful environment.

10. Keep relating to the same unhelpful people.

11. Put more importance on being right than on changing.

REFERENCES

Andreas, C. (1996). *Core transformation: Reaching the well-spring within.* Moab, UT: Real People Press.

Carnes, P. (1990). Personal communication.

Dabrowski, K. (1964). *Positive disintegration.* Boston: Little, Brown.

Gottman, J. (1995). *Why marriages succeed or fail: And how you can make yours last.* New York: Simon & Schuster.

Gross, T. (Interviewer). (2004). *Fresh Air* interview with Ken Tucker.

Guiliani, R. (2002, October). Interview on *Oprah.*

Gurganus, A. (1997, fall). Interview by Donald Antrim. *Bomb.*

Haley, J. (1991). Personal communication.

Hendrix, H. & LaKelly Hunt, H. (2004). *Getting the love you want workbook.* New York: Atria.

Lamott, A. (1995). *Bird by bird: Some instructions on writing and life.* New York: Anchor.

McMillen, J. C. & Fisher, R. H. (1998). The perceived benefits scales: Measuring perceived positive life changes after negative events. *Social Work, 44,* 455–468.

O'Hanlon, B. (2003). *A guide to inclusive therapy: 26 techniques for respectful, resistance-dissolving therapy.* New York: W. W. Norton.

———. (2000). *Do one thing different.* New York: HarperCollins.

———. (2006). *Pathways to spirituality.* New York: W. W. Norton.

O'Hanlon, B. & Hudson, P. (1994). *Love is a verb.* New York: W. W. Norton.

O'Hanlon B. & Hexum, A. (1991). *An uncommon casebook: The complete clinical work of Milton H. Erickson.* New York: W. W. Norton.

Pritchett, P. (1998). *New work habits for a radically changing world.* Dallas, TX: Prichett and Associates.

Seligman, M. (1998). *Learned optimism: How to change your mind and your life.* New York: The Free Press.

Watzlawick, P., Weakland, J., & Fisch, R. (1974). *Change.* New York: W. W. Norton.

Whyte, D. (1999). *Footsteps: A writing life* (audio CD). Langley, WA: Many Rivers Press.